"Dawg Gone... Movin' On!"

An Interactive, Multi-Generational Devotional Book Inspired by Pets and Places

By

**Chaplain (COL)-R Harold T. Carlson
&
Rev. Charles J. Carlson**

Xulon PRESS

29 Sep 08

Frank & Myrtle,

Thanks for your interest in our book.

I think you'll enjoy it.

McCoy R. Tinnick

Preface

—⚭—

We asked some of our siblings, friends and acquaintances to read our manuscript after it was completed and, if they wished, give us some feedback that we might include in these pages to whet your appetite for the devotional book we've crafted.

Our second sister, Ruth Arlene Carlson Phillips, who is a poet and the Executive Secretary for Robert D. Phillips, Architect and Innovative Greenhousing Systems, Inc. (www.igsgrows.us) penned the following poem as her contribution and view of us.

Empathy footprints
Sized to denote
the measure of weight they displace
Empathy faceprints
sure to commingle pleasure with pain
leaving gentleness
marking a visible grace
Empathy heartprints
A family legacy choosing to emulate
By poignant outreach extend
Tim and Chuck, action figures
They're tender toward plights
to deal with despairs 'til they end

A word-smithing duo
of mirth and wit teaching
They break into smiles
or a song on a whim
Internal or audible, tempered or not
their charm touches chords in us all
Uncommon occurrence
these two brother soul-mates
Given to all faith requires
We celebrate fully audacious tenacity
I recall first-hand their notable empathy

Ruth Arlene Carlson Phillips

DEPARTMENT OF THE ARMY
HEADQUARTERS U.S. ARMY CORPS OF ENGINEERS
WASHINGTON, D.C. 20314-1000

June 7, 2007

Chaplain (COL)-R Tim Carlson
9619 Hwy AH
Huggins, MO 65484

Tim,

The devotional book sounds great. I enjoyed reading day 29.

I'd be delighted to provide an acknowledgement...Here goes:

People say the world is getting smaller. Truth is, we are getting more mobile. The days of living in the same place for your whole life are pretty well gone. And then there's the transient life of the military. Chaplain Tim and his brother Chuck capture what it means to be a "sojourner" and "stranger" in the land. Dawg Gone, Movin' On will give you God's perspective and spiritual insight as you deal with loss and change. Who would better know the effects of these experiences than an Army Chaplain. This devotional book will comfort and encourage you as you walk with Jesus through hard times. To Tim and Chuck I say, "Well done!"

Van

Take care my friend

Essajans —

Dawg Gone...Movin' On! has touched the heart strings of your older brother too. So many stories I have known smatterings of, but many are new and so inspiring. Touching the heart with the truth of God's Word through good writing and sincere transparency, you both have captured the essence of God's power to use change and grief to move us closer into His embrace.

I have wept reading these marvelous devotionals. Many lives will be touched by this precious recounting of God's hand in the loss of your pets and the loss of your homes. I read six devotionals each day, and fourteen devotionals on Fridays. It's just my habit. These devotional stories you two have written, are second to none of them; I read devotionals from great Christian men and women who have written over the past three centuries.

Each of us needs to learn what God has taught you both— that times of trouble and sorrow and darkness are permitted by God to teach us lessons we desperately need to learn. God can use almost any method to teach us, if we have ears to hear Him. We all would like to avoid having to learn some of these necessary lessons. But the truth is the truth. Premature deliverance perhaps would circumvent God's plan in grace to educate us. You both have learned to abide in darkness knowing God is ever present. As the familiar saying goes, "It is better to walk in the dark with God than to walk alone in the light." Your journeys will lead others to discover God's grace in Jesus.

Moving the hands of a clock to suit us does not change the time. So each of us needs to learn the lessons your devotionals are teaching. We must not ever interfere with God's plans or with His will. Touching His desires touches His glory. That we must never do, for it mars His work. We can help a butterfly out of his cocoon, but our efforts spoil the creature. God's mills grind exceedingly slowly, but exceedingly fine. Your beautiful stories make that truth abundantly clear. Thanks for being faithful to remember and to use scripture to back up your lessons. I love you both.

Your brother,

Pastor Richard P. Carlson, Superintendent, Intermountain West District, EFCA, and Senior Pastor, Rock Springs Evangelical Free Church, Rock Springs, Wyoming

Acknowledgments
by Charles J. Carlson

—ɷ—

Honestly, it is hard to know where to start. I'm sure that I'll likely miss someone. Nonetheless, I'd like to thank my mother, Verma Elnora Granlund Carlson Larson (who left this world for a much better one in 2001), for blazing the trail by writing so many inspiring devotionals and choruses that so effectively communicated her faith to others. Thanks Mom for the inspiration. I would be remiss if I didn't also acknowledge my beloved father, the late Rev. Harold N. Carlson, for the impressions he left on my life. He passed away in 1966, when I was young. I wasn't too young to know that he crafted sermons, wrote poems, told stories and communicated the gospel, to people of all ages, with finesse, conviction and grace. We'll all meet again one day.

I'd like to thank all my siblings as each of them has helped to mold me into who I am today. Almost all of them have written extensively and have been published in various forms. Thanks then go out to Marilyn, Ruth, Rich, Tim, Bruce and David. I couldn't have finer siblings as each of you has been my life-long friend.

I'd like to thank my son Chad, who never tires of my stories or I of his! Thanks Chad for being an inspiration and an encouragement to me. I love you!

I'd like to thank my friend, Dr. Tom Rakow, for his friendship in our mutual ministry efforts when we were both pastors in neighboring towns in Minnesota. I frequently recall your belief, suggestions and prayers that I would put my thoughts together in 'book form' to bless others.

I'd like to thank my wife, Nicole, who has challenged and inspired me to keep writing. She has been the subject of several love poems (yet unpublished) that I've written in the past couple of years. She has also encouraged me to complete a tribute to my step-father and his 1969 Chevrolet pick-up entitled <u>The Incredible Life of Powder Blue</u>.

Last, but certainly not least, I'd like to thank my brother and co-author of "<u>Dawg Gone...Movin' On</u>" for giving of his time and efforts to edit carefully each page of our manuscript. Tim, you are a blessing! Thanks for your part in making this devotional possible.

Acknowledgements
by Chaplain (COL)-R Harold Timothy Carlson

—ᴍᴍ—

My mother, Verma Elnora Granlund Carlson Larson, instilled within me a love for grammar and a passion for writing. Mrs. East, my sixty-seven year old English Teacher at Clinton High School in Clinton, Iowa, taught me grammar and that she did very well. These two ladies have imprinted my personal and professional life in powerful ways. Deepest thanks go to you Mom and also to you, Mrs. East.

The United States Army Corps of Engineers, in concert with the Chief of Army Chaplains, chose me to be the first ever chaplain for the Corps in 1998. Not in two hundred and twenty-four years had the Corps ever had its own chaplain. While serving as their chaplain, I was given the opportunity to write an article in the 'Engineer Update' with a monthly readership of 40,000. Having this opportunity spurred within me a growing desire to write. That continues to grow and certainly has been instrumental in my decision to co-write a devotional book dealing with loss and change.

Since my father's death in 1966, I have been a sort of surrogate dad but more so, a special older brother to my 'baby' brother Chuck. While serving as the Installation Chaplain at Fort Leonard Wood I would often chat with my 'Bro'. Chuck has been a special inspiration to me and has encouraged me to join him in this endeavor of writing. Many thanks Brother!

My wife, Judy Raye, is my special encourager and polished content critic. Nothing lacking substance is looked upon fondly or easily accepted. Hence, my grammar takes a back seat to 'story line'. This way of writing, challenging real-life disclosures, has been invaluable. Sweet Jude, thanks a million.

Finally, I thank God for Jesus Christ who has given to me many talents. But most of all, I have a love for life and a passion for ministry to Soldiers and to their families.

Chaplain (COL)-R Harold Timothy Carlson

Contents

—ᗰ—

"Dawg Gone... Movin' On!"

An Interactive, Multi-Generational Devotional Book Inspired by Pets and Places

Introductions

—ᗢ—

This devotional book is a collaborative writing effort of two brothers, the now retired Chaplain (COL)-R Harold T. Carlson and Rev. Charles J. Carlson. Being born in different decades, each brother experienced life, love and loss in his own unique way. Our intent is for you and your family to use our book as a tool for interesting discussions during devotional times with your spouse, children, extended family and friends.

TIM'S INTRODUCTION:

It was twenty months ago now in May of 2005. One of my favorite times of any work day was the time I would dial my youngest brother Chuck. I would pull out the little mini writing drawer from my large mahogany, military desk. Then, I would put up my right foot and savor a time of chatting with my sibling. By the grace of God, I was the Installation Chaplain of Fort Leonard Wood, Missouri. I had over sixty persons who worked directly, or indirectly, for me in religious and morale support. But this time of the day was mine. I allowed myself to become lost in playfulness, verbal jesting and brotherly encouragement.

One day we broached the subject of devotions and devotionals. Since Dad died nearly forty years ago, my youngest brother had kept a special place in my heart. Being only ten at the time and I nineteen, I sometimes saw myself as sort of a surrogate father or caring Uncle to him. Chuck mentioned that he had lost thirty-one dogs in his lifetime and I replied that Judy, I and our family had moved at least that many times with our military life and the one that preceded it. "We should write a devotional book", my brother told me. It should be engaging and invite discussions around a family's dinner table or in a living room or family room. It would capture segments of our lives linked with one of Chuck's dogs or a place that we had lived. Then, with scriptures as a foundation, we would weave a true story relating to our life with our pet or place where we had lived.

A certain sort of light dimly shone, but the glow never really extinguished itself. Now, over sixteen months into retirement, living with my lovely wife Judy Raye, my son Kristian and my daughter Elizabeth, both grown, we are adjusting to life in the Ozarks on our two forty-acre properties. We would like to think, at least my wife and I, that this is our launching pad to heaven. We have moved a lot. But, we know that the scriptures tell us plainly in Hebrews 11 that many of the heroes of faith, in fact all, died awaiting Christ and heaven. But the insight is that they had some God-implanted awareness that heaven was their true home and that the human journey, here on this globe, will be one with many losses and the need for moving on.

Chuck and I are both ministers of the Gospel. I am in retirement after serving nearly twenty-six years as an Army Chaplain. In the earliest inscription days of my life, I also served for two years as a Chaplain Assistant. Chuck is away from the pastorate at present and currently working in the mortgage loan business. I received the 'Golden Quill Award' from LTG Ballard, the Commander of the Corps of Engineers in Washington, D.C. in 1999. In the spring of 2000, stemming from one of my articles on 'Servant Leadership' included in my column in the monthly 'Engineer Update', I was also awarded the Army-wide 'Keith L. Ware' Bronze Award. Chuck has his own accolades and was a stellar student at all levels of his education. We both enjoy words and sparring with grammar. We yearn for your finding errors and bringing them to our attention!

But more than any of the above, we believe that our contribution of this devotional book will be an encouragement to the Christian Community. Many good devotionals exist and we certainly commend them. Ours offers a unique focus upon losses, pressing on and learning that for all Christians, 'Heaven is our home'!

Chaplain (COL)-R Harold T. Carlson (Now, just Tim)
United States Army

CHUCK'S INTRODUCTION:

For those of us that are pet lovers, especially dog lovers, you will likely either love or hate my portion of this devotional book. Some of you might even think that because of the fates that some of my pets met, I (Chuck) never deserved a pet or cared properly for the pets I had. If that is what you think, it couldn't be further from the truth.

This devotional is, for me, first a tribute to the dogs that I've had so far in my fifty plus years of life. To date that number is 31 dogs and that seems far too many! Just like people, pets have their own unique identities and they bring so much into the lives of the families that love and care for them. I wanted to share some of the blessings that these animals were to me and to my family. More importantly, this devotional book is a tribute to my now forty-nine years of Christian faith which have sustained me through each and every joy, grief or loss that I've ever experienced. It also has helped me to be able to 'move on'. My life experience is the groundwork which I have used to become an author and published poet.

This devotional book isn't necessarily a 'feel good' one. It deals with the harsh realities of life including unwanted moves, accidents, sickness, death, grief and loss. With the exception of losing a parent, child, loved one or any other person of significance to us, there is little else that compares to the grief and loss that we can experience when a pet, that we love, dies or when we must leave a place and its friends behind. All of us have had to cope with the feelings these absences create. Hopefully some of our stories will encourage and inspire you. We trust that you find, as we have, that God can bring some good out of the most difficult circumstances of our lives. We believe that this devotional will help to encourage discussion about difficult life circumstances and perhaps help others to learn how to cope better with grief and loss, including the loss of those people, places or pets that were closest to them.

I (Charles) come to this topic with a great deal of experience in the world of grief and loss. The 'people' loss in my life has been tremendous. It would take far more than a mere devotional book to share my story. Unfortunately, I have also lost a ridiculously large number of dogs in my life. Yet, each one of them still has a piece of my heart. They are both the joy and the sorrow that brought this devotional to life. I have chosen fifteen pets to showcase in this devotional; but all the others could just as easily have been included.

If it were up to me, all dogs would go to heaven! The opportunity for people to go there is much clearer. As believers in Jesus Christ, we will meet again where the pains from our losses will be no more and where we won't ever think again about grief or moving on!! May God richly bless you, your family and your friends as you read, reflect upon and ponder our devotionals.

Rev. Charles J. Carlson (Chuck to most people)

Day #1
"Our First, Little 2nd Story Bungalow Apartment"

By Chaplain (COL)-R Harold T. Carlson

—ɯ—

Biblical Theme: Others' perceptions of us are less important than how God sees us and how He wants us to see our circumstances.

Scripture Verse for today:
1 Samuel 16:7b "For the Lord seeth not as man seeth; for man looketh on the outward appearance, but the Lord looketh on the heart."

It really was a cozy apartment. Nestled near to significantly higher dollar dwellings, 733 Osterman, Deerfield, Illinois, not five blocks from the Sara Lee Bakery, was the first place Judy and I ever lived as man and wife. It was 1969. We had just graduated from Trinity College nearby. Both Judy and I thought that teaching would be our lives. Judy held out for a high school job. She turned down a junior high offer. She became a waitress that fall as jobs for teachers began to tighten. I still had my student teaching to do. College, in many ways, had been easy for me. I took a lot of credits but I had not determined that doing my best was my first commitment. Self, sports and the opposite sex, one girlfriend at a time, had been my consuming passions. I was the "Most Valuable Player" on the basketball team and had a 23 point per game scoring average. The attention I received from this and from being the second best tennis player on campus meant so much to me then. I saw myself as so much more than I was! When the reality of graduation from college, coupled with a teaching job without any coaching began to sink in, I was disillusioned and inwardly quite distraught. I endured student teaching and barely got a 'C' average. But all of this is only preparatory to our life at our first apartment.

Maybe the rent was $100.00 per month. Maybe it was a bit more. Most of the furniture had come with the place. Our entrance was from outside. We would walk up a flight of stairs and enter the little living room with its slanted roof. Then we would pass into a small kitchen with a bath off the same little hallway. Then there was a sort of sitting room with the only other room being our bedroom. After work each day, Judy would come home in her waitress outfit. She was beautiful (still is) and the Deerfield Restaurant was lucky indeed to have her working for them. From her white little apron, worn over her black skirt, she kept her tips. She would empty her pockets, either on the kitchen table or on the bed. Then, we would count her daily intake. Ironically, she made at least fifteen per cent more than my $6,900 per year salary as a beginning high school teacher in nearby Wheeling, Illinois. But, without any doubts, I was embarrassed about our meager dwelling. I wanted others to think of this basketball 'star' and his prize, young wife as living in nothing less than a brick home with a lovely yard and no cares imaginable to restrict the acquiring of those things that defined so much of the North Shore's culture at that time.

Our family, thirty-eight years later, that now includes six children and ten grandchildren is most hospitable. My wife is a stellar cook, a great hostess and a fun person who makes others feel heard and recipients of special care. The early culinary skills, at our first home, were developing rapidly but our reaching out to others was absent. Within a few weeks of marriage I could tell that Judy was sad. More than once she cried. This was not her way. Even today she cries infrequently. Looking back, I think she was lonely and wishing that we would be more willing to reach out to others and tune to their lives. I also know she would have loved to have invited people over to our small place.

That quaint bungalow, that is no more, could have been a wonderful center for sharing Christ's love, for having a small Bible study group, for sharing a game of Rook or Apples to Apples...you name it. Sadly, I can only recall one or two instances during that year of our tenure when we had anyone over as our guest. I was embarrassed of our tiny home.

Have you ever been there? Are you there now? Are the externals more important to you and to me than those things that matter most....those things that really matter to God? "Man looks on the outward appearance, God looks on the heart". Are we willing to see our homes through God's eyes?

Questions for today:

1) Can you recall the first place you lived? Describe it.

2) How did you feel about your first home?

3) Are you able to value people more than places or does appearance matter more to you than relationships and the sharing of the story of Jesus Christ?

4) Is there any change that you would like to make that could encourage you to see the world in a manner more in line with the way God sees it?

Prayer: Dear Lord, I'm sorry I was so shallow when I first got married. I know the reason. I had chosen ways of sin and selfishness over a life of dedication to you. Thank you for your patience with me. Thank you for my godly wife and wonderful family. Thank you that I am learning to see things your way. In Jesus' name, Amen.

Day #2
"Mitzi...the Fight Instructor"

by Charles J. Carlson

—⁓—

Biblical Theme: Sometimes It Is OK to Fight!

Scripture Verses for Today:

Ephesians 6:10-17 "Finally, be strong in the Lord and in his mighty power. Put on the full armor of God so that you can take your stand against the devil's schemes. For our struggle is not against flesh and blood, but against the rulers, against the authorities, against the powers of this dark world and against the spiritual forces of evil in the heavenly realms. Therefore put on the full armor of God, so that when the day of evil comes, you may be able to stand your ground, and after you have done everything, to stand. Stand firm then, with the belt of truth buckled around your waist, with the breastplate of righteousness in place, and with your feet fitted with the readiness that comes from the gospel of peace. In addition to all this, take up the shield of faith, with which you can extinguish all the flaming arrows of the evil one. Take the helmet of salvation and the sword of the Spirit which is the word of God."

I'm sure that others in my family could do the story of Mitzi more justice. You see, I'm the youngest of seven children and Mitzi was 'their dog'...long before she was 'mine'. I am still impressed how this little dog taught her puppies to stand up for themselves in their own world. She evidently knew what many of us either already know or should soon come to realize...that life isn't always easy and sometimes it's ok to fight for what is right! It's even ok to defend ourselves!

Mitzi performed a valuable function for our family. Not only was she the family pet, but she was also a contributor to the family income. She was a purebred Boston Terrier. Her purebred puppies became a source of income supplement to our large family. Mitzi wasn't all about 'work' though for she was a blast to play with. She could retrieve, play dead and perform many other tricks too. My brothers had even trained her to bounce a ball on her nose.

Even though she wasn't very big, she was protective of us and of her pups. As a mother, she was consistent. We saw her teach each litter of pups in exactly the same way. Her pups only stayed with her for a few weeks and then they were sold to some other lucky family; but her mothering instinct drove her to teach her pups a valuable life lesson.... that 'sometimes it's OK to fight!! Pups don't open up their eyes right away. But not too long after they did, she'd grab one pup at a time by the scruff of its chubby little neck. Then she'd carry it out into the backyard. It was there that we were fascinated by her teaching methods. She would bark at the pup, dart back and forth towards it and then, when it wasn't looking, she'd quickly grab it by the back of the neck and either bite it or flip it in the air like a toy! If the pup whimpered but did nothing, she'd repeat the exercise. But if the pup became wise to her advances and barked back at her or swatted her with its paw, she seemed satisfied that it had learned to defend itself.

As believers in Jesus Christ we often hear teaching about being 'peacemakers' and about the importance of not fighting with others or not defending ourselves. There are some valid examples of those teachings in scripture. However, as you may have read in the passage of scripture recommended for today, we are also encouraged to fight against and protect ourselves from the enemy of our souls. The writer of Ephesians made it clear that our struggles are not really with those around us, but rather with and against the principalities, powers and rulers of evil in the heavenly realm.

Just as Mitzi taught her little ones to fight back, so also our heavenly Father instructs us on how we should 'fight back'. Keep in mind (if you are a parent, a grandparent, an uncle, aunt, brother, sister, or friend) it's never too early to teach the younger ones in our lives about a Godly defense against sin and the enemy who wants to destroy us. We only have the opportunity to influence others for a short period of time. Let's strive to be faithful teachers of truth to those with whom we have the opportunity to share our faith.

When our family moved from Kentucky to Iowa in 1964, my parents made the decision to leave Mitzi behind with family or friends. I was seven years old. This was the first time I had to deal with the loss of a pet and it was not an easy time for me. I wish I could say that I understood and adapted to this change quickly; but I didn't. However, I still remember, as if it were yesterday, what a great family pet she was and what wonderful life lessons she taught me.

Questions for today:

1) Do you remember your first pet?

2) What, if any, life lessons did you learn from having your pet?

3) Can you share a time that you felt that God was your protector and defender?

Prayer: Dear Lord, thank you for the many opportunities you give us to be positive influences in the lives of those we love. We pray that you will remind us often of the importance of defending ourselves against the one who seeks only to cause us harm, grief and pain. Thank you, Lord, for being our best defense. Amen.

Day#3
"Thinking of Others at 1260 Reaney"
by Chap. (COL)-R Harold T. Carlson

—ɱ—

Biblical Theme: We need to discipline our minds to think about others and their needs as much as we think about our own needs.

Scripture Verses for today:
Phillipians 2:3,4 "Don't be selfish; don't live to make a good impression on others. Be humble, thinking of others as better than yourself. Don't think only about your own affairs, but be interested in others, too, and what they are doing."

It's been an unusual day for a somewhat driven person like me. I was finally settling into the task of crafting another devotional. The thoughts had been bombarding my mind for a couple of weeks. The springboard, from scripture for this writing was, as I recalled it, "Think not only of your own things, but also on the things of others." Truthfully, there may be a translation that uses the word 'think'. However, and much to my consternation, I could not find the verse. Then, just as I was reaching a point of gathering angst, I heard the lovely voice of my wife, Judy. "Tim, could you help me to open some of the boxes in the garage?" Of course I could but the real question for me was, "Do you want to open those boxes now?" Definitely, I did not. Still, something about the key verse was playing upon my mind. I got up from the computer, headed for the garage and began to cut open ten to twelve of the moving boxes. We just retired five months ago and we are still moving into our place. Have you been there?

That wasn't all. I also had other missions. The heating element in our oven was broken. I also needed to get my car re-licensed as well as spend some quality time with our daughter, Elizabeth, our special child of twenty-eight years. Bottom line: circumstances urged me to think not only of my own things, but also upon the things of others.

Now, some six plus hours later, I'm home. My missions are complete and I actually found the Bible verse, thanks to my older brother, also a minister. Rich said, "Isn't the passage you're seeking the 'kenosis (Christ emptying himself) one? If it is, the word isn't 'think'; it is look". Sure enough, it was look. Nonetheless, the conveyance of meaning was a parallel track for sure. Armed with what I needed, I proceed now to tell my story.

It was 1970. I had finished my first year of teaching. I would give myself a low C. Maybe my classes would have given me more but I just hadn't linked with being a teacher. Judy and I thought that a move to the Twin Cities of Minnesota, her home, would be a great tonic. Of course this meant a move from our little second story apartment. From that there was little, if any, grief.

Both of us were in a sort of unreality bubble. We thought that the schools of Minneapolis would be eager, even yearning for our talents. The truth was that teaching jobs were scarce and finding one was not possible for us. That was not our first concern. You know the deal. One can live with relatives for a short time, but soon a couple needs a place that they can call home.

We were blessed to have my wife's family so tuned to our needs. Her sister, Marilyn Eastep, her husband Jack, Judy's parents and a few other family members secured an apartment for us on the East side of Saint Paul. 1260 Reaney was our new address. But, they not only obtained the upper duplex apartment; they thoroughly cleaned it. They installed carpeting. They painted. Their work, on our behalf, was the same as if they had been moving into the place.

What a delight it was for us to arrive from Deerfield, Illinois and have a living arrangement that gave to us autonomy and yet, closeness to Judy's parents and family. I was very touched. My life, especially since I was nearly seventeen, had been one of striving and seeking to attain laurels to embellish my sense of self and invite accolades from others. I did have quite a list of achievements but they seemed so little as I arrived in Minnesota. Who really cared about my being the 'Most Valuable Player' on the Trinity College Basketball Team? Who cared about the scholarship I turned down to attend Trinity in the first place? I was receiving a dose of reality and the baptism, at times, was very painful. But to Judy's family, my wife and I were 'dignitaries'! They cared for us and were willing to hyperextend to make us welcome and 'at home'.

As I reflect back upon those days I think to myself, "Where are you today, Tim? Are you thinking and looking to the things of others as much as you are looking and thinking to the needs of yourself"? I admit I am growing and God is at work in me. We have more than we need and our eyes aren't closed to others. Two weeks ago my son, Kristian, age 25, came home. He shared, with conviction and concern, that one of his workmates had just experienced a house fire. She was married to an Israeli soldier. "What are their greatest needs?" my wife asked. "Well, they need clothes the most", Kristian said. Her husband was just my size. I have rarely felt better than I did when Kristian came home a couple of days later and reported that the large garbage bag of clothes I gleaned from my closet fit this man perfectly. Apparently, he gave a sort of fashion show to his wife and was sincerely grateful. I could have used the clothes that I gave away but not as much as this man needed them.

How many other opportunities are right at our doorstep? Are we tuned to the needs of others? Are we willing, like my kind relatives, to look also after the affairs of others? I believe that such a demonstration of Christian love will change our world and incline others to God, his love and the great salvation found in Jesus Christ the Lord.

Questions for today:

1) Have you ever had someone or group of persons prepare a place for you and your family so that, upon arrival at your new destination, your home was ready?

2) Have you ever thought about a place, just for you, that Jesus is preparing?

3) What do you think it will look like?

4) Can you recall the last time that you thought also about the affairs of another or others and really made a difference in their lives?

Prayer: Dear God and Loving Heavenly Father, thank you for Jesus. He was willing to lay everything in heaven aside and come to earth because He knew how desperately we needed Him. Help us to tune our minds and hearts to Him, to others and to their affairs. Move us beyond thinking of just ourselves, our families, and our needs. Allow us to share the delight of another's joy because we heeded the words of the Apostle Paul and really thought about the needs of others. Finally, thank you for preparing a place for us. It must be a really nice place tailored just for each one of us. Awesome! Thanks, Lord. In your Holy Name we pray, Amen.

Day #4
"Duchess' Devotions"
by Charles J. Carlson

—⚏—

Biblical Theme: Time Alone With God Is Important, and Not Just On Sundays

Scripture Verses for today:

**Ps. 146:1-2 "Praise the Lord, praise the Lord, O my soul. I will praise the Lord all my life; I will sing praise to my God as long as I live."
Ps. 147:1 "Praise the Lord. How good it is to sing praises to our God, how fitting to praise him!" Deut. 11:18-19 "Fix these words of mine in your hearts and minds; tie them as symbols on your hands and bind them on your foreheads. Teach them to your children, talking about them when you sit at home and when you walk along the road, when you lie down and when you get up."**

One of the main reasons that we wrote this book was to remind others of the importance of personal and/ or family devotion times. Now some of you might not be familiar with this concept of 'devotions', but it is simply a time set aside personally or as family or friends to read God's word, pray, maybe sing praises to God and then be challenged, instructed or inspired for the day. There was so much that was communicated to us at family devotion times.

When we grew up, we had a 'family devotion time' like this nearly everyday, if not twice each day. Now that's a lot of devotions! In our world today that is so quick paced and frenzied, some families don't even get the chance to eat together on a regular basis nor do they seem to find other ways to meaningfully connect with each other throughout the week. Not only is it important to feed our physical bodies but we are all spiritual creatures and we need to find ways to feed our spiritual selves as well. It is our hope that this devotional book will help to inspire some awesome times alone with God or some great times of sharing in your family or circle of influence. We know, from experience, that by spending time together with those who are important to you, your relationships with them and with God will grow stronger.

It was after our family moved from Kentucky to Iowa that we got another pet. She was supposed to be a pet for the whole family, but in truth she seemed to be more our Mom's dog. She was a tiny Rat Terrier but as full grown as she'd get when we got her. She was already very established in her ways and one would think that it would have been hard to teach an older dog some new tricks; yet Duchess was very smart and she learned many things about us and about Mom's discipline very quickly.

Mom and Dad firmly expected that when they planned 'family devotions', you better be there and you better be attentive. In a family with seven children, you might well imagine that just gathering all of us in the living room or around the kitchen table was quite an accomplishment. No doubt it was. The first few times we had devotions with Duchess, she learned some valuable lessons. The first thing she learned was that when the family sang, she couldn't bark, and if she did, she'd be sent to the back porch where it was cold and lonely. It wasn't long till she mastered not barking at inappropriate times. The next thing she learned was that during devotion time, she wasn't the center of attention... God was. She was famous for going from lap to lap looking for someone to pet her. This was great for her but very distracting for us kids. We just didn't seem to pay attention like we should have when she did this. So once again she was sent to the porch to patiently wait for our time to be over.

Mom, who had a tender heart towards the dog, soon gave her another chance to be part of our devotion time. She allowed Duchess to sit next to her on the piano bench, and if she did so without moving or disturbing anyone, she was allowed to stay. It wasn't long until Duchess learned what was expected of her so that she could hang out with the rest of us.

However, the most amazing thing Duchess learned at devotion time wasn't taught to her by anyone, but rather what she taught herself. Not long after Duchess received the place of prominence beside Mom on the piano bench, she began quietly observing our family. It is unbelievable what we can teach to others, even pets by example! When Mom or Dad would tell us it was time for prayer, we'd all bow our heads, close our eyes and fold our hands to pray. I'm not sure how long it took her, but soon we were all amazed that when we bowed our heads, closed our eyes and folded our hands, she'd do the same. That little dog somehow understood and mimicked us. This was forever her position during prayer time. It was here that she'd nuzzle close to Mom... she'd close her eyes as if she were praying...she'd keep her slightly tilted head down to one side and then she'd cross her paws as if she wanted to talk with God too!! It was another sad day for my family and me when Duchess was no longer able to be part of our family devotion time. Her absence left more holes in our hearts.

Today's reading includes scriptures that challenge parents to teach and to train their children in the faith. My parents not only did that quite well in our home, but they also taught our pets what they needed to know to navigate within our family system. Truly, if a little Toy Terrier can learn to take time out of its busy day to spend time with God, maybe it's not too much to ask of ourselves, our children, or those in our circle of influence. You'll be amazed at the spiritual rewards that will come your way when we put God first!

Questions for today:

1) Did you grow up in a family that had 'family' devotions?

2) What did you like or not like about that?

3) What is one way that you could share your faith with someone you love?

Prayer: Dear Heavenly Father, thank you for loving us and wanting to spend time with us. We pray that we would always want to spend time with you too! Help us to make time for you and help us to experience these times without the many distractions that can come to disrupt and to discourage us. In Jesus' precious name we pray, Amen.

Day #5
"Camp Zion"
by Chaplain (COL)-R Harold T. Carlson

—⟋⟍—

Biblical Theme: We need to learn to make our temporal dwellings into places that anticipate and welcome "Zion, the home and eternal abode of our great King, Jesus Christ, and all who love Him."

Scripture Verses for today:
Psalms 48:1-2 "How great is the Lord, and how much we should praise Him in the city of our God, which is on His holy mountain! It is magnificent in elevation, the whole world rejoices to see it! Mount Zion, the holy mountain, is the city of the great King!"

Hebrews 11:8-10 "It was by faith that Abraham obeyed when God called him to leave home and go to another land that God would give him as his inheritance. He went without knowing where he was going. And even when he reached the land God promised him, he lived there by faith-for he was like a foreigner, living in a tent. And so did Isaac and Jacob, to whom God gave the same promise. Abraham did this because he was confidently looking forward to a city with eternal foundations, a city designed and built by God".

I could blame my mother. She was alive in 1971. My dad died in 1966. My draft number was low and that was not good. It was number 51. So, two days before my twenty-sixth birthday, not attaining the magic age that would have exempted me from military service, I arrived at the 43d Reception Station at Fort Leonard Wood, Missouri to begin a sojourn that spanned nearly twenty-eight years.

While I was experiencing becoming a Soldier, my wife Judy, nearly five months pregnant, was also having a sort of Basic Training. She had to decide what to do while I was away. Her decision, a sage one I opine, was to get an apartment near to her folks but to retain autonomy from them during my time of training. Her choice of home was a few rooms above a garage that she shared with friends of hers. The name of that place was Camp Zion. How could such a small property (1566 Furness located there on the east side of Saint Paul, Minnesota), that included a home and garage with an apartment above it, be called 'Camp Zion'? Well, tell the Peters family that had this property over thirty-five years ago that they just might have misnamed their acreage. I'm certain that they would laugh and say, "Oh no, that's exactly what its name was and should have been."

Usually when I think of Zion, that little spot doesn't come to mind. Instead I think of the Zionist movement, which began in the early 1900's when the Jewish exiles began their return to Israel. This people group was first deported from Israel in 721 B.C. by the Assyrians. Later, Judah was taken into exile by the Babylonians in 596 and later 586 B.C.

I am reminded of the significance of Jerusalem and how Jews today still speak of 'going up to Jerusalem, to Zion'. The concept of 'Zion' is also important to Christians. The words of an old hymn come to my mind. "We're marching to Zion, beautiful, beautiful Zion, we're marching upward to Zion, that beautiful city of God". To my mind back then, and still to my thought processes now, 'Camp Zion' at 1566 Furness was simply not Jerusalem. It wasn't Jerusalem and so it certainly wasn't 'heaven' either! Yet to those who named it, it was 'Camp Zion' with all that this idea conveys.

I never really lived at the camp. My camp was much different. I was a member of Echo 3-3, Smoke and PT (Physical Training), the best d--- company in the BCT (Basic Combat Training), or at least we were told.

Truth is, Judy and I knew that I was headed for Viet Nam. After all, we had a war going on and conscription was alive. In Basic we sang 'Jodie' calls like "Saigon River, Saigon River, four more rivers to cross, hey, four more rivers to cross". We sang other songs like, "I want to go to Viet Nam, I want to kill 'ole Charlie Cong". Some were much better as the list of calls went; some were much worse. (As an aside….We are a cleaner Army now but the need for God and for chaplains and chaplain assistants is strong. Could God be calling you?) Thankfully, Vietnam never happened for me. President Nixon's decision to stop sending troops in January of 1972 changed my assignment from 'Nam' to Fort Leonard Wood, MO.

To this day, all Basic Training Soldiers are forced to take leave from mid-December to early January because of the Christmas and New Year's Holidays. This time period is curiously called 'Exodus'! When I returned at Christmas for this break, my wife and I spent most of our time, if not all, at her parent's home. I have no significant memories of Camp Zion. But still, that place has a special place in my mind for two reasons. The first is that it was home to my precious wife at a very vulnerable time in our lives. The second is simply the unusual name it bore…Camp Zion.

As I think about the thirty or so places that we have lived, I am reminded that the world is too small for all of us. We are creatures for eternity; we are headed for 'Zion'. Our homes, whether small apartments or large farm dwellings, like the one we now inhabit, are but sojourning structures. Growing up, we often sang songs like "Oh they tell me of a home far beyond the sky, oh they tell me of a home far away, oh they tell me of an unclouded day!" Perhaps you remember other verses too just as I do. But this business of being pilgrims, even foreigners is linked to the name of the place where Judy lived in 1971 and early 1972. Yes, Camp Zion is an invitation to you and to me to make our current dwellings heaven friendly. How about it, are our homes overtly welcoming Zion? Is the décor within our homes one that invites us to muse about our eternal dwelling? Oh, I know it's highly unlikely we should be naming our street 'Zion' or our house 'Camp Zion'. But still, I think we can share a certain anticipation, an intentional futuristic inclination to lean into the idea of God's preparing a special place for us. It's so special that whether an earthly mansion or a flat above a garage... Zion truly beckons. Have you ever thought of such things?

Thirty-five years later, Judy and I now thank the Peters Family for naming their modest property 'Camp Zion'. Wow...what a repository of reflection, spiritual meaning, eager anticipation and a reminder that Jesus is preparing Zion for you and for me, children of His; because we have received his forgiveness and asked him into our hearts and lives.

Questions for today:

1) Can you remember your third home? What was it like? Do you ever miss it?

2) Can you think of ways to make your current home a place where people feel welcome but also think about our heavenly home?

3) Are you willing to pray for Jerusalem and for God's people? They are the 'apple of His eye' and I want them to be in heaven too. (Another little aside....While serving as an Army Chaplain for nearly twenty-six years, I would periodically have persons of the Jewish Faith question my praying in Jesus' name. I finally decided that I would say that my best friend was Jewish. In fact, He was Jesus the Lord. As I think about this, I also know that He is the one who told his disciples, "I go to prepare a place for you." I believe the Zion of which we have mused, the city which captured Abraham's imagination, is this very place. In my heart I know that all the world needs to know this great Savior, Architect, Engineer and Creator who is making our eternal Zion.)

Prayer: Lord, help me to learn to live like Abraham. Give to me the faith to value the home I have but incrementally release it so that your Zion will grow in my mind and my anticipation of my life with you for eternity will be encouraged by pointers that reside in my current dwelling. Thank you for the people who have helped me to think of matters of eternity like the Peters Family. Walk with me this day and together, we will come to Zion! Amen.

Day#6
"Lucky, the Name That Didn't Fit"
by Charles J. Carlson

—w—

Biblical Theme: Names Are Important to God, He Has A Special Name For Us!!

Scripture Verses for today:

Proverbs 22:1 "A good name is more desirable than great riches; to be esteemed is better than silver or gold."

Rev. 2:17 "He who has an ear, let him hear what the Spirit says to the churches. To him who overcomes, I will give some of the hidden manna. I will also give him a white stone with a new name written on it, known only to him who receives it."

Rev. 3:5 "He who overcomes will, like them, be dressed in white. I will never blot out his name from the book of life, but will acknowledge his name before my Father and his angels."

When it comes to naming our pets, most of us take the responsibility seriously. We want our pet to have a 'cool name' and we hope that our pet lives up to its name. The truth is that sometimes the name we give our pet just doesn't fit or doesn't work out the way we thought it would. My dog 'Lucky' was a shining example of this.

49

We discovered him at the local dog pound. He was the last pup left of an unwanted litter. I was certain from the start that his name should be 'Lucky' because he was lucky to be alive and I was lucky to have found him. I knew what it had been like to live without a pet, so I took my puppy chores very seriously and I rarely missed a detail. One of the first things that we got for Lucky was a wooden doghouse. I carefully lined his new home with a rug, a small blanket and some 'puppy appropriate' toys. Basically, Lucky had it made! I played with him first thing every morning, most every afternoon after school and spent lots of time with him on the weekend. I knew that he was going to be a great pet.

That first month spent with our family flew by and Lucky grew like crazy. On one cold and snowy morning, my mom gave me some warm milk to add to his regular breakfast menu. She even let me take a small piece of burnt bacon along for him. It paid to be 'Lucky' and he was living like a king! I put on my coat, mittens and hat and went outside for our typical morning romp. As I got past the back porch, I started calling him. "Lucky...Lucky...come here boy. Hey, breakfast time! Come Lucky, come! He didn't come and at first I was worried that he had somehow gotten off his collar and chain and had run away. But soon I was relieved to see his chain coming from his dog house...just the way it was supposed to be. Then I figured it out. Lucky was simply playing a game of 'hide and seek' with me. That seemed harmless enough so I called him a few more times and then I'd had enough. It was cold outside and I needed to get ready for school. "Ok buddy, I found you"! I yanked lightly on the chain but Lucky didn't come bounding out like usual. So I pulled a little harder and I felt him move but he still wouldn't come out. So finally I pulled vigorously on the chain and when I did, I pulled a dead frozen puppy from his resting place.

There wasn't much consoling my eight year old brain for several days following that trauma. I just couldn't believe what had happened and couldn't accept that even though I'd named him "Lucky" and even though I'd taken such good care of him and we had this great relationship, he really wasn't "Lucky" after all! I learned that "just because we are called something, it doesn't mean that's who or what we are or who or what we will become"! I learned this truth works both in the 'pet world' and in the 'real world' too.

Now when it comes to naming our children, most of us parents take that responsibility even more seriously. We want them to have a great name and we hope that they will live up to the name that we give them. However, once again we have to accept that just because we name our kids 'a particular name' that depicts a certain blessing or attribute we desire for them, it doesn't always mean life turns out that way for them or for us. Yet 'name giving' remains one of the joys of parenting. Unfortunately there is often another type of 'naming' that happens with many of us. The opposite of 'name giving' is 'name calling'. Many of us have or will experience this in our childhood homes, schools, neighborhoods and sadly, even in churches. It would be wonderful for those who resort to name calling to realize that it just isn't true that 'sticks and stones can break our bones but words can never hurt us'. In fact, sometimes those 'name calling' events bring back frustration, anger or grief many years later.

I grew up in a family of seven children. Five of us were brothers; I was the youngest. My parents didn't tolerate name calling by any of us. However, our parents weren't always around to monitor or protect us so I too received a share of teasing from my brothers. One time after one of these sessions, I went to my mom and complained to her about all the names that my brothers had been calling me. She made it clear to them that they could no longer call me any of these 'bad' names. So after that, they didn't! They did something much worse instead. When they knew she wasn't around and they really wanted to get to me, they'd simply call me

'Names'! They'd taunt me with 'Names, Names, Names' until I'd cry. I just couldn't take the remembrance of all those ugly names flooding my mind! Remember, 'name giving' is meant to be fun, but 'name calling' is not!! Thankfully, just because someone calls us 'someone or something', it doesn't mean that's who we are or what we will become!

There is a 'naming' that's even more important than naming our pets or our children. Did you know that our heavenly Father also enjoys 'name giving'? In fact, for each of us, He has planned a name for us known only to Him. It's a special name meant only for us and it's a name that no one can ever take away from us nor can we ever lose it because of some bad behavior or unfortunate incident in our lives. His special name for us is likely a name that describes who we are in His eyes and who we have become because of our loving relationship with Him. Look again at the scripture verses for today and be encouraged by the name God has for you. The only thing you have to do is believe on Jesus Christ as your Lord and Savior and then you will never lose it. You can do that by asking Jesus Christ into your life. When you do, He will forgive your sins and give you an eternal home and a name that can never be taken away from you...even if you've been a 'name caller'!! This biblical truth is meant to encourage us and should make all of us feel 'lucky', loved and blessed!

Questions for today:

1) Do you like your name?

2) Did anyone ever call you names?

3) How did you deal with that?

4) For what would you like to be remembered?

Prayer: Dear Heavenly Father, thank you for being with us during hard times in our lives, like the times when we lose our pets or have had to struggle with the names that others have called us to hurt or to wound us. Please help us to be kind to those around us and forgive us for those times when we haven't lived up to the name that we've been given. Help us to remember how much we are loved and that one day, if we accept you as Lord and Savior, we'll get a new name that no one can take away from us. Amen!

Day#7
"Jerry-Rider and the Attic"
by Chaplain (COL)-R Harold T. Carlson

—⟶

Biblical Theme: Husbands love your wives.

Scriptures for today:

Proverbs 25:24 "It is better to live alone in the corner of an attic than with a contentious wife in a lovely home." Ephesians 5:28 "In the same way, husbands ought to love their wives as they love their own bodies."

Have you ever moved three times or lived in four places? Our fourth place was nearly an attic apartment. I was a 'Jerry Rider' for four or five weeks in early 1972. (Jerry-riders live in New Jersey and commute to New York City to work). Each day I would leave the lovely suburb of Teaneck, New Jersey, cross the George Washington Bridge, go into New York City and ride down the eastern edge of the Hudson River, go under the channel through a tunnel and arrive at Fort Hamilton, NY. There I was training to become a Chaplain's Assistant.

I remember one day looking at a wharf and seeing a ship almost bigger than one's imagination. There she sat-the Q.E. II, the Queen Elizabeth II. What a contrast to the life in Queens, the Bronx, and Brooklyn. More than once I would see a stalled car in the morning and by the evening when I returned from training, it had been completely stripped of tires, radio and sometimes even the engine! But, living in our apartment on the third floor of a lovely, older, large home in New Jersey was pure pleasure. Why? Some reasons are obvious when one compares life with that of the inner city. But the major one was that, while in Advanced Individual Training for the United States Army, I had my wife Judy with me and we had our own apartment.

So you might just be wondering, "When will he tell us how contentious Judy really was as she neared delivery of his firstborn daughter?" Truthfully, those days never came. My time could indeed have been an attic one with a crust of bread but God blessed me with a companion and friend. She was willing to risk a long drive to the East Coast and live in a third story apartment with several flights of stairs just to be together rather than living alone in Saint Paul, Minnesota.

I remember the view from the window. We could see such tranquility. The houses reflected varied measures of wealth with established living styles marked by nice lawns, newer cars and apparent peacefulness. What a contrast this was to the inner city.

The first suggested scripture for today brings thoughts to me of a man, beleaguered and worn, tired from quarrels with his wife. He has retreated to the highest level of his home. There he sits, hidden in a corner, with a crust of bread and perhaps a glass of water. I see a man in hiding, a soul searching for some calm from his storm. This has not been my lot.

What makes a wife so difficult? Are some men just victims of troublesome women? Perhaps these men, who eat crusty bread in lonely places, have forgotten their mandate to 'Love your wife even as Christ loved the Church". I recall some years ago reading that if we treat our wives like thoroughbreds, they will never become 'old nags'.

So how are things for you right now? Is your home happy? Do you have an upper story apartment with the simplest of furnishings? Do you have a really nice, big, even sprawling mansion? But even more important, are you enjoying life with your spouse? Do you share your lives? Do you eat together and dream together?

Judy and I paid a price to live in New Jersey. The Army didn't recommend it. We really couldn't afford it. But, upon reflection, we'd never do it differently. We were working at getting to know each other, at learning about financial, geographical, military, community, church and new friend challenges. It was a time of growth, risk and most of all, a time to lean upon God to find how we could more fully understand His great love for us and our commitment to love each other.

Yep, life as a 'Jerry-Rider' left its impressions. One of the best memories for me is remembering the great meals from that lofty height with the wife of my youth. That woman, whom I love, remains Judy Raye Nelson Carlson. No attic crusts for me!

Questions for today:

1) Are you living in your fourth place? How long have you lived there? Do you like your neighborhood?

2) Have you ever sought a secret place to eat because you and your wife have been quarreling?

3) (For the children hearing this devotional) Have you ever hidden from your family because they were being mean to you?

4) On a scale of 1-10, with 10 being the highest, how would you rate your marriage? Are you seeking to follow the challenges of Ephesians 5:21-32?

5) Do you know someone who is struggling in his or her marriage? Will you pray right now for them?

Prayer: Dear Lord, thank you for our high apartment in Teaneck. Thank you for helping us to better love each other in those early, vulnerable years. Thank you for keeping our '67 Pontiac GTO in good working order so that it was not stripped on the Hudson Parkway. Thank you Lord for the gift of my wife, my soul-mate, my companion and friend. Help me to never take her for granted or treat her so that she becomes a nag. Help my wife and me to reach out to other couples and to share with them your love. May we also be real, honest and transparent about our growth edges. We pray this prayer in your most holy name, the name of Jesus. Amen.

Day #8
"Rover and His Watchful Eye"
by Charles J. Carlson

—⁓—

Biblical Theme: God Keeps A Watchful Eye On Us; We Are Also To Be Watchful As We Wait for His Imminent Return!

Scripture Verses for today:

Psalms 121:3-8 "I lift up my eyes to the hills-where does my help come from? My help comes from the Lord, the Maker of heaven and earth. He will not let your foot slip-he who watches over you will not slumber; indeed, he who watches over Israel will neither slumber nor sleep. The Lord watches over you; the Lord is the shade at your right hand; the sun will not harm you by day, nor the moon by night. The Lord will keep you from harm-he will watch over your life; the Lord will watch over your coming and going both now and forevermore."

Matt. 26:41 "Watch and pray so that you will not fall into temptation. The spirit is willing, but the body is weak."

I Tim. 4:16 "Watch your life and doctrine closely. Persevere in them, because if you do, you will save both yourself and your hearers."

One of the interesting things about pets is that sometimes other people's pets can come to mean just about as much to us as our own pets do. This was the case with my brother-in-law Paul's dog, Rover. Rover was no ordinary pet; he was a 'working dog'. Paul had gotten him as a puppy and he'd trained him to be his 'farmhand'. I developed a deep appreciation for Rover and as odd as it is, he is the only dog that I've ever been close to that has died of old age!

I was ten when my father died and what was left of our family moved from Iowa to South Dakota. I bonded almost instantly with Paul and he became my 'substitute' father. Bonding with Rover took more time. Paul was the very best thing to having my own dad around and I will forever be grateful for the love, time and attention that he gave to me. I liked spending time out at their farm and I soon was deeply enthralled with everything about farming. It was here that I developed a 'working relationship' with Rover. He tolerated me but he truly loved Paul. He'd let me pet him but he'd play with Paul. When I called for him, he rarely even perked his ears, but when Paul called him...he flew into action!

Rover was an English Shepherd...mostly black with distinctive white markings on his neck, tail and paws. He also had some brown coloring around his eyes. Speaking of eyes, Rover was getting older and he'd lost one of his eyes to disease or perhaps a dog fight defending his territory around the farm. So unfortunately, Rover only had one very watchful eye. As I told you earlier, Rover was a working dog. His breed is known for being great 'cattle dogs' and Rover was no exception. One of his jobs on the farm was to help herd the cattle as they grazed the roadsides in the summer-time. Paul would bring Rover up to the corner at the end of the mile road just one-half mile north of the farm place. Then he'd turn the cattle loose and they'd graze the ditches. When they got near the intersection, Rover would bark like crazy and this would always turn the herd around and head them back towards the farm. Then he'd wait right there and watch carefully until the cattle had gotten to the other end of the road about one-half mile south of the driveway. Here Paul would be waiting in his car to once again send them back to Rover. This cattle herding process could last the whole afternoon. When I came to work for Paul, it seemed that Rover could keep his end of the bargain almost by himself, but I was the one who needed help turning the cattle back towards home. It amazed me how watchful and attentive Rover was, even with just one eye!

This was only one of the many jobs that Rover had on the farm. Another task that he did, nearly everyday of his farming career, was to help Paul do the chores. Again, to do this job, he needed his 'watchful eye'. His job was to keep the cattle from getting out of the feedlot gates as Paul hauled their feed from the silage pit to their feed bunks...one slow moving tractor loader scoop at a time. Paul would open up the gate and with complete trust in Rover, he'd take off on his tractor. Rover would then sit down in the middle of the open fence line. Paul didn't ever have to remind him to 'stay', 'sit', or anything. Rover just knew his job was to wait and to watch! It didn't take long for the cattle to realize that Rover meant business. If any of them got near the open gate, Rover would bark and chase them away. Nothing deterred him from his task. As I think back about Rover, I have realized that this dog could teach us all a thing or two.

Have you noticed that we live in a society today that hates 'waiting'? We want 'what we want', when we want it. We have instant everything from 'credit' to 'oatmeal'. We have drive-up banking and fast food. The idea of us simply 'waiting and watching' seems repulsive to most of us. Yet in the scripture readings for today, we are reminded of the importance of watching for the imminent return of our Lord and Savior Jesus Christ. Much like Rover, we too are called to always keep a 'watchful eye' out so that we are aware of everything that is going on around us. In fact, it's one of the most helpful suggestions given to us for our daily lives. While we are watching and waiting, we can and we should be working as well. We can work to head off temptations when they get too close to us and send them back from where they came. We can work by standing watch at the gate of our hearts and minds. In doing so, we can resist and repel the things that would lead us away from God and from going down the wrong paths. I challenge you to take your job of waiting and watching seriously, as seriously as Rover did.

Questions for today:

1) What is the hardest thing for which you wait?

2) If this were the last day of your life, what would you do?

3) Is there something you'd like to tell someone in your family that they should be careful about or for which to be watchful?

Prayer: Dear Heavenly Father, we want to thank you for your watchful care over us. We need to remember that you could return to take us to live with you forever, at any time. Help us not to be so caught up in our daily activities that we forget to be active 'waiters and watchers'. Help all of us to see the opportunities that you bring to us each day to help you to build your kingdom. In Jesus' name, Amen.

Day #9
"We Too Were Poor"
by Chaplain (COL)-R Harold T. Carlson

—ᚱᚱ—

Biblical Theme: We need to be 'tuning' to the poor.

Scripture Verses for today:

Proverbs 22:22 "Do not rob the poor because they are poor or exploit the needy in court. For the Lord is their defender. He will injure anyone who injures them."

Proverbs 21:13 "Those who shut their ears to the cries of the poor will be ignored in their own time of need."

Jeremiah 22:15-16 "But a beautiful palace does not make a great King! Why did your father, Josiah, reign so long? Because he was just and right in all his dealings. That is why God blessed him. He made sure that justice and help were given to the poor and needy, and everything went well for him. 'Isn't that what it means to know me?', asks the Lord."

I really don't know abject poverty. I know of it and I cannot reconcile the plight of the poor in a way that gives me lasting peace. In 1970 Judy and I served as short-term missionaries in Zaire, Africa. The Mbaka tribe lived very simply with mud huts and sleeping mats made of native woods. Sticks were gathered each day, by women and children, for the necessary fires to make the rice, millet, or corn that had been ground the 'old fashioned' way, which was by using a weighted stick or device that looked like an upside down handle of a garden pick. They plunged it repeatedly into a hollowed out log that held the grain. In spite of this kind of lifestyle, this was not poverty.

Orphans living in the sewers of UlaanBaatar, Mongolia, where my daughter and her husband David Arnegard served for three years, is poverty. Or children abandoned and left to live in cardboard boxes and eat whatever can be found on the streets or in the dumps of Peru is poverty.

Nonetheless, our fifth dwelling was a most meager one. By any standard of American poverty, we were poor in early 1972. We rented the place in Waynesville, Missouri. It was 402 Washington. There is still nothing to commend this place. Sadly, I heard that some twenty-five years later, someone was murdered there. But back then, we were just beginning my first tour in the Army after my Basic and Advanced Individual Training. I was now 'Permanent Party', as they called it. The walls were cheap paneling. The bathroom walls were stained. The lighting was dim. The bedroom was just a sort of box and the yard was the parking space plus Missouri rocks and dirt on a sloping hillside. How poor were we? The Army had just raised basic pay from @$96.00 per month to @$218.00 per month. There was a housing allowance of @$100.00 per month and a modest, yearly clothing allowance. There were good dental and medical benefits but after paying rent, buying food and stretching the budget to pay the gas for my 'Goat' ('67 GTO), money was tight. So, often I would ride to work with the other renter of the duplex, Dan Burson. Dan had a motorcycle and it got @100 miles per gallon.

One day Dan came by to pick me up for our eleven mile ride back home. As we passed the Post Exchange he exclaimed, "We're out of gas!" That was before the days of twenty-four hour gas stations in the area and we were in a pickle. We pushed the cycle back to the station but the pumps were closed. I commend, to this day, his initiative. He took every pump hose, leaned it to the ground and drained any remaining gas into a can. There was enough to get us going and off to a station less than five miles away that could 'fill'er up!' Yes, by American standards our life at 402 Washington was a baptism into poverty.

So much has changed for me. The installation, at which I was a Private making @$300.00 per month as a Soldier, is the same installation to which I returned thirty-one years later as an Army Colonel. My pay, with benefits, just last year exceeded $120,000.00 per year. But, as I reflect back upon those earliest days, I think of God's protection and provision for us. Our first child, Alida Raye, whom I mentioned was a missionary to Mongolia and now, soon to China, was born. Our neighbors were Christians and good friends. We were able to pay our bills. We had food on our table. We were surrounded by caring chaplains, assistants and chapel attenders who loved us and extended Christian kindness. We were the 'poor' who had God as their protector. I thank God for our fifth home. Our sojourn there was short but the memories and spiritual lessons still remain.

Are you poor? Are you unemployed? Has it been a hard month or two in your business where sales, and sales alone, give you the needed commissioned income that sustains you? Are you a Christian? Do you believe that God's Word remains as true today as it did over twenty-six hundred years ago? At that time Jeremiah told us that God looks after the poor. He also told us that those who truly know him, and are blessed with earthly goods, will be tuned to the plight of the poor.

Questions for today:

1) Do you think about the poor?

2) Do you consider yourself poor?

3) Do you believe that God is your protector?

4) Have you ever moved four times? Is there a place you'd rather be?

5) Are you hopeful? Do you believe that God is still looking out for the poorest of the earth?

Prayer: Dear Lord, Thank you today for the memories of 402 Washington in Waynesville, Missouri. Our times there were not ones where we felt hungry or needy. That was because You sustained us, provided our food and protected us. Thank you for such care. As you observe the sparrows, and even know when one falls, surely You know where we live, what we need to wear, what we need to eat and how we will meet our current financial obligations. Open our hearts this day to those in need. Help us to have hearts like King Josiah, who was always tuned to justice and caring which he extended to the poorest of his land. We pray this prayer in Jesus' precious name, Amen.

Day #10
"Spike, The Grief Counselor"
by Charles J. Carlson

—ᴍ—

Biblical Theme: God Is Always Our Best Source of Counsel.

Scripture Verses for today:

Ps. 73:24-26 "You guide me with your counsel, and afterward you will take me into glory. Whom have I in heaven but you? And earth has nothing I desire besides you. My flesh and my heart may fail, but God is the strength of my heart and my portion forever."

Isa. 28:29 "All this also comes from the Lord Almighty, wonderful in counsel and magnificent in wisdom."

John 14: 16, 26-27 "And I will ask the Father, and he will give you another Counselor to be with you forever."

If I had to choose which pet that I'd want to see in heaven some day, it would be Spike. He was a beautiful dog. As a unique blend of Saint Bernard/German Shepherd and Collie, he was 'monstrous' in size but as gentle as a lamb. In my estimation, he possessed the very best qualities of each breed. Spike is extra special in that he holds my personal record for 'the pet that lived with me the longest'. He was in/briefly out/then in my life again for a total of ten years. If I were to write a book about just one dog, I would write about

Spike. It isn't easy to limit my descriptions of him and our relationship into one, simple devotional.

As I write now, I am again reminded that when Spike died unexpectedly while I was in college, I took three days off from school to grieve his loss. In fact, I wrote both poetry and prose in his honor. I've searched my files extensively and I just can't find my writings from 30 years ago...imagine that! Even without what I wrote then to aid my memories, I can still recall fondly his beautiful fur coat and markings. I can remember his playful ways, his bark, his smile, his 'kisses' and his love of 'dancing' on his back legs. I was astonished at the enormous amounts of food that he could consume in record time. Mom always said he 'ate like a horse'!

About two years after he came to live with us, we were forced to give him away because our neighbor girls got scared when he 'danced' with them. Luckily, we gave him to the man who would eventually become my step-father (which is a whole story in itself). Spike quickly acclimated to the farm and he loved country life. I can picture him in the front seat of our powder blue pickup with the wind blowing in his face. I remember him sitting as if he were on a kingly throne as he nestled comfortably beside me on the tractor platform as we 'took the fields by storm' completing the necessary farming tasks.

Perhaps my musings about Spike have opened up some memories for you about your own favorite pet. I don't think we should ever belittle the importance that a pet can have in our lives. A pet can be so many things to us. My dog, Spike, fulfilled many roles for me including, but not limited to, being my best friend, playmate, confidante, protector and in perhaps his most important role, my grief counselor. Admittedly, those are big shoes to fill, especially for a dog!

In the 1960's there wasn't nearly as much attention given to the field of counseling nor were there as many opportunities for it as there are today. People were much more inclined to 'live with' whatever 'issues' they had and just make the best of it. Certainly counseling wasn't the multi-billion dollar a year business that it is today both inside and outside the walls of our churches. In truth, I probably could have benefited from a little counseling help back then, but instead I was given the gift of Spike!

My father passed away in May of 1966 when I was ten. Even though I came from a large family, the days following my dad's death were very lonely times for me. Our family moved from Iowa to South Dakota within a month of the funeral. I immediately left behind the security I thought I had, including my school and church friends. Again, when we moved, we left behind our pets with whoever promised them a happy home.

My transition into small town life in South Dakota wasn't easy, so when my oldest brother Rich got wind of how things were going for me, he decided that what I needed most was a 'friend' that would be around me every day. It was an excellent plan as Spike was the biggest, cutest, most responsive puppy I'd ever seen. We bonded instantly and for life! We were inseparable as he became the first thing I wanted to see in the morning and the last thing to see before I crawled into bed at night. He became the one that I could laugh with, cry with and basically tell ALL my true feelings about losing my dad or about how I felt about moving to another state with different kids, a strange church and new school. He was my grief counselor and he did an amazing job. It was nearly impossible to be 'down' when I had someone as exciting and fun to be with as he was. No matter what the weather or my mood, Spike was always an attentive listener. When he would lay his head in my lap, I felt like the luckiest person in the world.

Even though he was 'just a dog', he instinctively knew one of the most fundamental truths about helping others when they grieve. The truth is that it isn't 'what we say' or 'how we say it' that's most important. Rather it's our presence with people at those times of grief that they will remember the most. Spike gave me the awesome gift of his presence.

It wasn't pleasant when I lost my 'grief counselor'. It opened old wounds and I was left to figure out what to do when our 'grief counselor' dies? Where are we to turn? Well, if we believe what we read in today's scripture readings, we'll realize that in spite of trying circumstances, we really have the best counselor of all available to us, all the time. God, in His ultimate wisdom, gives Himself to us to be our wonderful counselor and our very best source of peace and joy. Pets are great, but God is the best!

Questions for today:

1) What is your fondest memory of your favorite pet?

2) When you have been grieving, who has helped you the most? What did they do?

3) Is there something going on in your life today that you want or need to share with God?

4) Is there someone around you that could use some encouragement or help with a difficult time of grief or loss?

Prayer: Dear Heavenly Father, thank you for being there with us at the most difficult times in our lives. Thank you for providing wisdom, guidance and counsel to us. Please help us to be open to sharing our grief not only with You but also with others who can be of help to us. Help us to see others who may need us or some other human 'with skin on' to be an encouragement to them. Amen.

Day#11
"Give It to Jesus"
by Chaplain (COL)-R Harold T. Carlson

—ɯ—

Biblical Theme: Give what you have to Jesus. He'll do the rest!

Scripture for today:

Luke 9:13-17 "But Jesus said, "You feed them". "Impossible!" they protested. We have only five loaves of bread and two fish. Or are you expecting us to go and buy enough food for this whole crowd?" There were about five thousand men there. "Just tell them to sit down on the ground in groups of about fifty each," Jesus replied. So the people all sat down. Jesus took the five loaves and two fish, looked up toward heaven, and asked God's blessing on the food. Breaking the loaves into pieces, he kept giving the bread and fish to the disciples to give to the people. They all ate as much as they wanted, and they picked up twelve baskets of leftovers!"

I can see her now, nearly thirty-four years later. There she sits in the backyard of our 72 Knight, Fort Leonard Wood, Missouri quarters. Yes, like the Jeffersons, we were moving on up. Whether it was the east side or the south side, our worst side, low life apartment in Waynesville, was over. The Army let me, a rather lowly Private First Class, move right next door to a Sergeant First Class. He was an E-7 and I was an E-3. We had never had a place so large and so nice. How large was it? Actually, it was probably 1300-1400 square feet with solid oak floors, a nice kitchen, with built-in dishwasher and great appliances for cooking and cooling. But Alida Raye, our first-born, had a special place that she loved. I had found an inner tub for an automatic washer. I placed it outside in our backyard. Into that container I would put Alida. She would peer over the top, smile, look at the world and not worry about wobbly legs and falling. She did not walk until she was twenty-two months old.

Another memory of this, our first ever United States Army quarters, was the scene of our weekly Bible study that we hosted. Soldiers and a few officers were seated throughout the living room and even stretched out and up the stairwell. At times, we had over forty persons in our home. It was an era of new praise songs. Speaking in other languages, which God gave to persons, was also much in vogue. Even the Catholic Parish had a book about 'elephants without a trunk'! This trunklessness, of course, referred to members of the parish who did not speak in tongues. I couldn't 'go there' because it didn't jive with my beliefs from I Corinthians 12-14 which would entail more than a devotional thought. But, nonetheless, we had some great singing.

One of our study members was a great song writer and he had a number of his works published. But, the remarkable thing about this home was that we gave it to God to use. It wasn't large really but the spiritual impact that God allowed had significant results. Couples came to know the Lord. Judy and I had our calling more cemented, even though it took eight years for my becoming an Army Chaplain to be realized. But, in many ways, we gave up our quarters to Jesus just like the young lad that gave his lunch to the Lord.

Where do you presently live? Do you have a Bible study in your home? Have you ever done such a thing? Do you have stories to tell about how Jesus is multiplying the gift of your home to extend the kingdom of God here on earth? To this day, nearly four decades later, we have friends that we met while I was a conscript at Fort Wood. These people are dedicated Christians who have given their lives to various avenues of Christian service. Yes, there are also sad stories. The writer of Christian songs returned to his lifestyle of homosexuality. That has been a very difficult matter. When I think of him, his wife and four children, I ache. I wonder, "Is he still alive?" Has he repented? What of his wife and family? Indeed, this is one of those 'tell it to Jesus alone' kind of agonies.

But, 72 Knight was a very special place to our family. Whether a vantage for Alida's viewing her young world from out of doors, or our having a huge crowd for an evening study of God's Word; this place was our 'loaves and fishes' experience. We gave what we had to Jesus and then let him do the rest.

Questions for today:

1) How many times have you moved? Were they hard moves or welcome ones?

2) Do you have special memories of God's working in your lives because you gave your home to Him?

3) Have you ever been part of a 'Home Bible Study' group? Would you like to be?

4) Do you feel part of a support group that really cares for you? If not, would you be willing for God to direct you to one?

Prayer: Dear Lord, thank you for the miracle of allowing us to receive government quarters when I was only a Private First Class. Thank you also for the gift of Alida Raye. What a treasure she remains, as well as her husband and their five children. Bless them as they prepare to return to work with the Mongolians. Help us to continue to seek your face to know if we should start another small group at our rural farm place? Give to each person who hears this prayer a heart to believe that, if we give our places to you, You will do the rest. May the part that You do be a repository of wonderment and glorious surprise. In Jesus' Name we pray, Amen.

Day #12
"Rex's Rejection"
by Charles J. Carlson

—ოა—

Biblical Theme: God loves us and will never reject us, if we believe in Jesus Christ.

Scripture Verses for today:

John 3:16 "For God so loved the world that he gave his one and only Son, that whoever believes in him shall not perish but have eternal life."

Romans 5:8 "But God demonstrates his own love for us in this: While we were still sinners, Christ died for us."

Romans 10:9, 10 "For it is with your heart that you believe and are justified, and it is with your mouth that you confess and are saved."

Eph. 1:13 "And you also were included in Christ when you heard the word of truth, the gospel of your salvation. Having believed, you were marked in him with a seal, the promised Holy Spirit, who is a deposit guaranteeing our inheritance until the redemption of those who are God's possession-to the praise of his glory."

If you haven't had to deal with today's devotional topic before, my guess is that you will have to someday. Most all of us have had or will have to deal with 'rejection'. The rejections of this life can be many and our reactions to them varied. Some of us were chosen last on the playground at recess; others were rebuffed in our dating years; some of us didn't get the job we wanted or were fired from a job; some of us didn't have our writings published; while others of us suffered rejections from friends, children, family, churches, and perhaps even our spouse. The bottom line is that rejections stink and few of us like them or know exactly how best to handle them.

When it comes to our pets, it seems that we can easily understand when we have to 'reject' a pet for whatever reason, but it's much more difficult when our pet rejects us!

That's exactly what my dog Rex did to me. We usually think about dogs being 'loyal' no matter what. However, it just isn't true...because you haven't met Rex!

After I was forced to send my favorite dog, Spike, to the country, my mom promised me another dog. After school, I used to play basketball on the playground with some of the other junior high boys. One day, one of the kids started talking about their dog and how she had given birth to a litter of five pups earlier that spring. They still had three of them left. The kid wanted to know if I knew of anybody who would want one. In truth, I was still grieving the loss of Spike, but I figured there was no better way to move on than to get another pet. I went with Joey to his house. He didn't live far from the school and I could easily pass his home on my way to and from school. For some reason, when I had, I hadn't noticed their dogs. There were four of them playing in the front yard. The pups were almost full-grown and there wasn't much doubt as to why Joey's family wanted them gone. Truthfully, they weren't the greatest looking little mutts in the world. I sat down in the yard to watch and play with them. The one with the most personality quickly caught my attention. His name was Rex. I called my mom at her workplace (which wasn't the greatest plan) and asked about bringing home a new dog. Reluctantly, she agreed. I took a piece of heavy string and made a leash. We set off happily for home.

Rex was some sort of short-haired Terrier cross. What he didn't have in breeding, he made up for in attitude. He instantly 'took over' our home. He wanted what he wanted when he wanted it. He was as smart as could be and very fun to play with. I really enjoyed his company, but Mom...well, not so much! I guess he was always underfoot when I was away at school and much higher maintenance than some of the other dogs we'd had. One day, when I was away at school, Mom let Rex out of the house to "do his business", but when she called for him a few minutes later to come back in, he wasn't around. To my surprise that afternoon, when school was out, Rex was waiting for me on the playground! I scolded him and took him home with me. From then on, we started putting him on a chain in the backyard everyday. No matter what collar we put on him, he seemed to figure out how to get out of them and he'd be waiting again for me after school. We should have named him 'Houdini'!

The truth was that I actually liked this new idea of having Rex greet me each day after school. Remember this happened in the late 1960's and the little town we lived in didn't yet have a 'leash law'. So it soon became a regular habit for Rex to accompany me to school in the mornings and hopefully be there to greet me when school was out. I never thought much about what he did throughout the day. Some days Mom said that he came back home to sit on the porch, but usually he was gone all day. She had no time to look for him so we both became accustomed to Rex just 'doing his own thing'. People who knew him said he walked around like he owned the town!

One morning on my way to school, I walked past Joey's house. It wasn't the way that I normally got to school. Rex saw his mother playing in their front yard. He ran to her as fast as he could and they greeted each other like old friends. I didn't see any other pups around anymore. I called for Rex but he wouldn't follow me. I didn't think much of it and I just kept walking on to school. That afternoon, when school was out, Rex wasn't there to greet me like normal. So I walked back to Joey's house and sure enough there sat Rex...just like he owned their place too! I called for him but he didn't budge. So I went up to the door and as I did, I noticed that he was chained to the railing. I rang the doorbell. Joey's mom came to the door. She kindly explained that most everyday Rex came by their house to play and that most every day they had been feeding him. She explained that since the other pups had been given away to other homes, Rex's mom just didn't seem to be herself. She wondered if maybe Rex wouldn't just be happier staying right there with them. I assured her that wasn't the case. I knew he'd rather be with me. I called him...he just sat there and wouldn't budge. He had rejected me! I was so frustrated that I just left him and walked home. That night as Mom and I talked about Rex, we came to the same conclusion that Rex probably was happier with his old family. In fact, for him it probably felt like he'd never left them! My mom called Joey's mom and the deal was arranged. I visited Rex from time to time but our relationship was never the same. I didn't appreciate his rejection of us but in time, I understood it.

Some people never recover from the rejections that they receive in life. It's sad, because all of us are loved by God and we should never wallow in our rejections. In fact, He loved us so much that He died to save us and to insure that we would never have to endure the ultimate rejection...separation from God for all eternity! Today's scripture readings remind us that we can be sure of God's love and we can be sure of our eternal destiny, if we are believers in Jesus Christ!

Questions for today:

1) Have you ever been rejected? How did you feel?

2) Have you rejected others and if so, why?

3) Have you asked Jesus Christ to be your personal Savior?

Prayer: Dear God, thank you for loving us enough to send your only Son Jesus to die for us and to save us from our sins. Thank you for the promise of eternal life with you. Thank you that you have promised never to leave us or to forsake us. Be with those of us who have suffered rejections. Thank you for always staying with us, even in those painful times. May we willingly share this good news with others, in Jesus' abiding name, Amen.

Day#13
"Learning to Walk"
by Chaplain (COL)-R Harold T. Carlson

—⁓—

Biblical Theme: Walking to God is the first step we should take in our spiritual lives and the last step we look forward to when He brings us to our eternal home.

Scripture Verses for today:

Proverbs 4:25-27 "Let thine eyes look right on, and let thine eyelids look straight before thee. Ponder the path of thy feet, and let all thy ways be established. Turn not to the right hand nor to the left: remove thy foot from evil."

It was a true milestone time of our lives. Alida, our firstborn, was eighteen months old at the time. She was closely tied to both of us parents but especially to my wife, Judy. When we left the Army, after finishing the required two years of a draftee, we decided to move to the Twin Cities, my wife's girlhood home. We located an apartment in a complex of newer ones on Lower Afton Road situated between South Saint Paul and lower east Saint Paul, Minnesota. It was a hard time in our early marriage.

I expected that getting some kind of a job in a metropolitan area would be easy. It wasn't. Early in our time there, we resorted to literally counting our coins, mostly pennies. We had less than one dollar and no employment as yet. Remarkably, on that very day, friends of ours from the Army whom we had met at Fort Leonard Wood, Missouri sent us a check for $80.00. It arrived on that day of near penury. Even more unusual was this: our friends did not practice 'tithing' (giving a tenth of one's income back to God). Retrospectively, God was demonstrating to us that He cared for us and that He would take care of us too. Judy and I were taking baby steps towards God. We were learning His ways.

My wife's friend, Lee Anne, had just opened a Day Care Center in Minneapolis as part of the 'Soul's Harbor' Inner City Church. She knew that Judy was an excellent teacher so she hired her as the Head Teacher for her center. While this solved some immediate money issues for us, it inverted our chosen paradigm of the husband's working and the wife's being the homemaker, nurturer and teacher of our child. All of this was unfamiliar and very difficult for both of us. With anguish, Judy accepted the job. I encouraged her to do so as living with nothing was impossible. I planned and hoped to find suitable employment as soon as I could, but this was something we simply had to have to survive.

The lingering memory from our Lower Afton Road dwelling remains our daughter Alida. She was pained to see her 'Mommie' leave each day in the early morning. She came to realize that she would not be home until late in the evening either. At this time "Alley Cat", as I often called her, had not yet mastered walking. For her, the months from eighteen to twenty-two were ones of learning to walk. I would sit across the living room near the couch and beckon to her. As she would begin her walk my way, it seemed that she would make it for sure. Most of the time, something would distract her and she would lose focus. Fortunately her 'path of learning' was not strewn with sharp edges or dangerous spots for injurious falls. Alida had great determination and together, forging a new relationship with her as the only present parent, she began to walk. This was a little by little...step by step time of our lives.

I think of the passage of scripture for today as I recall those days of our daughter's learning to walk. "Let thine eyes look right on" comes first to my mind. As I would look into Alida's eyes, adding my paternal encouragement, she would stay upright and continue moving towards me. As I noted, she would often become distracted and look away. Maybe she was internalizing her progress and feeling kind of coy and able. But at those moments, she would lose her balance and "bam", down she would go. I would lift her up, look into her eyes and urge her to take those remaining steps to my outstretched arms. Is this not an example of Jesus' way with us, His children? How often do we forget to look straight ahead? How often do we become distracted? How often do we fall?

As I think a little further in our text, the words "ponder the way of thy feet and thy way will be established." I doubt that Alida gave any consideration to such thoughts back then. I do know that as Christians this admonition is sage indeed. If we take this 'word' to heart, we will save ourselves from countless hours of regret, sadness and heartache. How are we now? That time, many years ago, was a 'learning to walk time' of our daughter's life. That was over thirty-three years ago. Since that time, this child is married...has three girls and two boys! I like the names that she and David chose for them; Kristina, Clara, Dorothy, Oskar, and Joseph. She has become the teacher and now all of her children can walk. But the path that she has taken to this point has involved countless points of path divergence. I know that there has been much pondering since those earliest days of learning to walk to and with her dad.

I will soon be sixty. I am now retired and days are much different. There is no idleness but there is more time to ponder what to do next. The challenge for me now, and for the remainder of my time on earth, is to ponder the way of my feet. Among the competing desires and demands, and the pleasurable events and fun; which ones will I choose? Which ones will bring me closer to my Heavenly Father's arms and safely home?

So then, will we all continue to refine our walking? Will we resolve to look straight ahead and ponder the way of our feet? "Walk with me, walk with me, lest mine eyes no longer see, all the glory, all the story of your love…" the song goes. Surely, before we can walk with Jesus, we must certainly **walk to him!** To do that, let's look straight ahead and with our feet arrive 'safe in the arms of Jesus, safe on His gentle breast.' After we have done that, He'll give us some further marching orders that will take us with Him and direct us deeper into His love and purpose for our lives.

Questions for today:

1) Your seventh home...Do your remember it? Do you recall the exact address?

2) Can you recall a neighbor's face or name? If so, do you still stay in touch? Was this neighbor a Christian?

3) Was there a particular challenge that you or your family faced while living at this location?

4) Would you consider one memory as more precious than any other as you recall this particular place of abode?

Prayer: Dear Lord, it's been awhile since we lived on Lower Afton Road. We both know that those apartments are now gone. Thank you for keeping our family safe in your arms and walking in your steps since then. Thank you also for demonstrating your love and care through that unexpected gift of money so many years ago. Be with all of our children today and especially, with Alida Raye. In your kindness, be with those parents who know that their children are walking, but not with You. May these children, many of whom are now grown, yield their lives to you and learn to receive your love and your marching orders. Be with our now grown "Alley Cat" as she and her family adjust to yet another new home in far away Monticello, Utah. Give to me the wisdom to pause each day and ponder. May this time of daily reflection create for us increased purpose as we journey farther into this life that you have graciously given. May your life and love be established within me so that I may touch others with hope, kindness and tender care. I pray this in the name of Jesus Christ my Lord, Amen.

Day#14
"Sheeba, Doing Right When It Hurts!"
by Charles J. Carlson

—ɱ—

Biblical Theme: Doing 'what's right' isn't always easy for us to do.

Scripture Verses for today:

Romans 7: 18b-20 "For I have the desire to do what is good, but I cannot carry it out. For what I do is not the good I want to do-this I keep on doing. Now if I do what I do not want to do, it is no longer I who do it, but it is sin living in me that does it."

James 4:17 "Anyone, then, who knows the good he ought to do and doesn't do it, sins."

Josh 24:15 "As for me and my household, we will serve the Lord".

After college, when my dog Spike passed away, I didn't really have a pet that I called my own. My folks replaced Spike quickly as 'every farmer needs a good dog'. The puppy they chose had some of the same markings as Spike but a totally different personality.

We never bonded. So I didn't chose to have a pet until after I had gotten married. In fact, the pet we had wasn't a pet that we chose, but a pet that chose us!

It was a beautiful fall evening when Mary, the wife of my youth, heard a strange, scratching sound coming from our back porch. We were 'stationed' at the Southeast South Dakota Experiment Farm where I was the livestock research manager. The farm was sprawling and the cattle feedlots and hog units were full to overflowing with the livestock that we were using to complete our various feed and animal husbandry trials. The only dog that typically came around the farm was my boss Fred's St. Bernard named Clarence. Clarence was as mean and as scary as any dog I'd ever seen. I frequently got chased on top of a parked car or into a safe outbuilding whenever Clarence unknowingly made his unwelcome visits to the farm. So when we heard the scratching, I went to the door fully expecting that I'd find Clarence there. In that it was long after working hours, I sort of welcomed the opportunity to voice to Clarence how much I disliked him and I hoped I'd get to chase him away with my verbal assault.

To my surprise, when I went to the door, Clarence wasn't there. In fact, I didn't see anyone or anything. So I gingerly stepped out the door and called for Clarence, but he didn't appear. With this, I went back into the house and settled into whatever TV show we were watching. Before long, the strange scratching sound was on our porch again. This time Mary volunteered to go to the door. When she opened up the screen door, in bounded a beautiful greyhound dog! The dog was very curious and before we could stop it, it ran up the open stairway and made its way from room to room. We were so surprised that we couldn't seem to think of what to do. The dog seemed pleasant enough and it wasn't demonstrating any threatening behaviors; so we just watched it and followed it as it explored this new world it had found. After a time of searching out our house, the dog went back downstairs and lay down on the kitchen floor. We slowly approached her to see if we could pet her. We could and did and she seemed to love us. Because it was already night-fall, we fed and watered her and put her in the closed front hallway. We figured we would try to find her owner the next morning.

The next morning, she seemed glad to see us. We had noticed that she didn't have any collar or tags that might help us in our search for her owner. We let her outside and she took off like lightning. I don't think I've ever seen a dog run so fast. She disappeared out into the open corn field and we figured she was gone. But in a few minutes, she was back and eager to get back in the house. She seemed to bond especially well with Mary. The dog seemed amazingly well housebroken so we knew she was someone's pet. By noon that next day, the dog had a name. We called her Sheeba. That night, we let her sleep with us at the end of our bed. We sort of forgot about looking for her owner. Besides, if someone was really missing her, they'd likely come looking for her soon enough.

Every evening for the rest of the week, we played with Sheeba both inside and outside on the farm. It was a treat to see her run like the wind. She was so well-behaved and friendly. By week's end, we had fallen in love with her but we knew that what we were doing just wasn't right. We hadn't even tried to find her owner. So reluctantly, we ran some small ads in the local papers. We also put up a few signs at places like the local truck stop and vet's office. We honestly felt we had been given a 'gift' but we knew we wouldn't feel good about keeping her unless we 'did what was right'. I assured my wife that most likely no one would call us...I was wrong!

Within a few days our ad appeared in the paper alongside a similar ad placed by someone looking for their dog. Their unwanted call came and we quickly made the arrangements with the owners for them to pick up their dog. It turned out that 'Sheeba' was really a racing greyhound that belonged to the owners of the dog race track in Sioux City, IA, about fifty miles south of us. She had somehow gotten loose after a recent race and they wanted her back. We accepted the small reward they gave us for our time and trouble.

We were astonished to find out that she had never been a house dog or anyone's family pet! She had never spent a day indoors 'til she met us. She had lived in a little kennel her whole life and the life she would be returning to probably wasn't that great. We figured they'd race her 'til she stopped winning and then she'd probably end up being someone's medical research dog. It wasn't a pleasant thought, but yet when I think of her, I am reminded that 'doing the right thing' is sometimes very hard to do. In fact, sometimes doing what is right just plain hurts!

Truth is, for all of us, everyday is filled with hard decisions. We have a lifetime of choices to make and a 'conscience' that can steer us in the right direction. More importantly, for those who are believers in Jesus Christ, God equips us with the presence and power of his Holy Spirit. We have been and will be given opportunities everyday to 'do the right thing'. We are all in the ultimate race to the finish. My hope and prayer is that we all finish well!

Questions for today:

1) Have you ever lost a pet?

2) What did you do to try to find it?

3) What is your most recent example of 'doing the right thing'?

4) What tough choices did you have to make?

5) What, if any, 'rewards' did you feel/get for doing what you knew was right?

Prayer: Dear Heavenly Father, thank you for seeking us out when we were lost. We praise you for giving us the Holy Spirit to guide us into all truth and challenge us to do what is right. Forgive us for the times when we have failed you. Help us to be willing to do what's right, even when it's very hard to do! Amen.

Day #15
"Bluebirds of Eternity"
by Chaplain (COL)-R Harold T. Carlson

—ɷ—

Biblical Theme: Houses on earth, regardless of how well built or how precious, are earthly and must pass away. However, we as the building blocks of God's eternal home, are created for eternity.

Scripture Verses for today:

2 Corinthians 5:1 "For we know that if our earthly house of this tabernacle were dissolved, we have a building of God, an house not made with hands, eternal in the heavens".

It finally happened in 1974. Judy and I purchased our first home. For some reason I do remember the address. It was 5237 10th Avenue South, Minneapolis, Minnesota. It was a stucco bungalow, well-built and situated among other homes of similar design. It's hard to believe but that home sold for $26,900. Our interest rate was 4 and ¾ percent and the monthly payment only $241.00. That was then.

Now my electricity bill is often greater than that! The amazing thing about this dwelling dawned one day when my nephew and I took a ride over to the 'old neighborhood'. There it was: 5237 10th Avenue South. That was in 2005. The home was for sale. It's price…$345,000.00. Amazing indeed! $345,000.00!!! Is there a financial lesson for the young here? I sold the property in 1977 for about $29,000.00

and I thought I had made a deal. Apparently I was much too hasty. However, this older home will not always continue to appreciate in value. It is earthly and hence must someday pass away.

The excitement in our household was great. I had 'bought' a job. I was tired of the prayers of the saints and felt like an object of pity. So, I went to an employment agency and became an insurance underwriter. This was not a match made in heaven. It did, however, afford to our family some good credit scores. Along with Judy's income as a teacher, the financing took place and 'voila!, we were homeowners.

We were just getting to know the neighborhood when restlessness, born of a different expectation, changed our direction. A little high school, now defunct, in southwestern Minnesota by the name of Verdi needed a coach and athletic director. Judy was pregnant and we did want a lifestyle where my wife was a true homemaker and I was the bread winner. You might have already guessed what happened to our 'dream home'. Yes...it became history.

One special memory lingers from that first home. My brother-in-law was a carpenter. He loved to tinker also. He would fix the bodies of rusted-out cars and was quite good at it.

However, in the summer of that first year of home owner-ship, he obtained a trailer. It barely fit into our space near the little garage, just off the alley. We extended ourselves in kind-ness so that Tim could try his hand at 'trailer restoration'.

Late one afternoon it happened. A young lady, with obvious high hopes of a life with my brother-in-law, came to help on the refurbishing project. I heard drills spinning and grinding noises. Then, came a sort of yelp or scream. She had somehow hurt herself and gotten something in her eye. It didn't cause blindness but it heralded the end of that relationship.

In a sort of metaphorical way their ill-fated, and short-lived time of dating mirrored our 'marriage' to this little dwelling. We only lived there from April to early November of that year. So quickly our dreams shifted. We left our home.

Have you had experiences like the ones I have mentioned? Have you had great hopes that a house which you just purchased or a plan that has just become reality would last? Have you been a person who thought you had just the perfect match but then your marriage has become a sad ruin in history?

Our earthly sojourn is a lattice of change. It is a cross-stitch of interruptions and altered plans. Do we actually understand this? Do we properly pause to reflect upon this life phenomenon?

Why does 5237 10th Avenue South have such poignancy to me over thirty-five years later? From a human perspective, it represents what could have been. I could have been over a third of a millionaire right now. I could have held on to something that I simply 'let go'.

But, there is a lasting observation that gently bombards my mind this morning. As I watch the sparrows pecking on my deck, I too am 'pecking away'and thinking of our God-link. Not one person, ever born, can ignore it. Our Creator made us to be creations of eternity. We are mysteriously building blocks in a structure whose Builder and Maker is God. We cannot escape this situation. We can, and often do, forget about this. Many of us tend to sell one home, buy another, build a bigger one and continue to grasp hold of our living places as if they were ours to keep. We can't. Whether we let them go too soon, as we did, or whether we keep them for a lifetime; they will never outlast us. We are the ones that are built to last.

Wow! The sparrows just left now and Missouri's bird, the Bluebird, just landed on my deck. Beautiful...!!! Actually there were two of them and they were amazing. Is it possible that the sparrow that we see in ourselves and others is more profoundly different and beautiful to God than these Bluebirds were to me this morning? Is it plausible that some grand sort of metamorphosis is closer in time today than 5237 10th Avenue South was to Verdi, Minnesota for Judy, Alida and me back in 1974?

We can't take our homes with us; not those built of wood and stone. Neither can we prevent God's taking us when our time on earth is through. Are we ready for that? Are we beating with hearts of faith? Are we ready to become 'Bluebirds' of eternity that no human eye has seen or fleshly ear has ever heard that can make adobe and brick easily forgotten. Will I see you in God's heaven? May it be so. Amen.

Questions for today:

1) An eighth home...Have you had one?

2) Lingering memories...What special one comes to you from that home? If you haven't had one, what do you think it would be like to move so many times?

3) Do you ever think of moving? Do you treasure the metaphor of human beings being building blocks within the house of God where Jesus Christ is the Chief Cornerstone?

4) What is better than a good house investment?

Prayer: Dear God, thank you for helping Judy and me to buy our first home. It truly was a 'honey'. Thank you also for placing within us a restlessness that gave to us the strength to leave our family and the familiar to follow You. Help us to remember those special days and to learn from them. While it is difficult to understand, thank you for shaping us into unique stones for the household of God. We relish glimpses of your plans for us and hints of eternity like the 'blue birds' that you showed to me today. We love you and marvel that You have made us to last forever. Thank you, God. In Jesus' Name we pray, Amen.

Day #16
"Isaac...the Dog that Didn't 'Heal'!"
by Charles J. Carlson

—ɯ—

Biblical Theme: Keep Praying, Keep Believing...Your Miracle Might Be Next!

Scripture Verses for today:

Ps. 103:1-5 "Praise the Lord, O my soul; all my inmost being, praise his holy name. Praise the Lord, O my soul, and forget not all his benefits-who forgives all your sins and heals all your diseases, who redeems your life from the pit and crowns you with love and compassion, who satisfies your desires with good things so that your youth is renewed like the eagle's."

James 5:13-16 "Is any one of you in trouble? He should pray. Is anyone happy? Let him sing songs of praise. Is any one of you sick? He should call the elders of the church to pray over him and anoint him with oil in the name of the Lord. And the prayer offered in faith will make the sick person well; the Lord will raise him up".

2 Cor. 4:8-9, 16-18 "We are hard pressed on every side, but not crushed; perplexed, but not in despair; persecuted, but not abandoned; struck down, but not destroyed. Therefore we do not lose heart. Though outwardly we are wasting away, yet inwardly we are being renewed day by day. For our 'light and momentary troubles' are

achieving for us an eternal glory that far outweighs them all. So we fix our eyes not on what is seen, but on what is unseen. For what is seen is temporary, but what is unseen is eternal."

Many dog owners take their pets to obedience school. One of the commands the dog learns is 'heel'. I wish my dog, Isaac, had learned to heel, but more importantly I wish he had been 'healed'!? Let me explain. After our encounter with Sheeba, the Greyhound, we realized how much we wanted a pet. We decided that we wanted a German Shepherd puppy and we wanted the enjoyment of seeing it grow up through its puppy stages. We watched the newspapers religiously and soon found our prize. Isaac was a beautifully marked purebred pup, the largest in his litter. Even as a pup, he had the most regal stature. He seemed to know that he was destined for greatness.

He had gigantic paws, a monstrous appetite and he shocked us as he grew like a weed. By four months of age, he appeared almost full-grown except for some gangly remnants of his puppy days. Sometimes as Isaac raced across the backyard, he would trip over his own feet, get all tangled up and tumble to the ground. He'd quickly get up and look around, as if pretending that nothing had happened. He was smart and had easily mastered all our 'housebreaking rules' and every other trick we taught him. He was friendly yet protective. He loved to play on the living room floor with us but mostly he liked to chase sticks, balls or anything we'd throw for him to retrieve. He had easily acclimated to both inside and outdoor life. We anticipated we'd have a long and happy life together.

One Sunday morning, when he was just six months old, we heard the most piercing whines I've ever heard, coming from downstairs in the kitchen where Isaac sometimes slept. I figured he really needed to be let outside so I bounded down the stairs. What I saw in the kitchen is still painful to think about. Isaac was standing on his back two legs with his large, overgrown paws up on the counter. As I took a closer look, I realized that both of his front legs were broken right above the joints of his paws. When he saw me, he had the most miserable expression in his eyes as he allowed himself to drop to the floor. His front legs were useless as he propelled his way towards me on the floor.

I called for Mary and we took him in our arms and we began to cry. I had already had a lot of loss in my life and I couldn't imagine that I was going to be faced with another one. We recalled that in scripture God is the 'healer'. We had been taught that God watches over all of us, even the animals. We decided to pray. We knew God could heal him. We had faith and we believed. We probably even bartered with God for his healing, making promises about our spiritual lives and our commitments to Him, to others and of course, to Isaac. Unfortunately our praying and pleading didn't produce any immediate results. God didn't heal him. Isaac was in obvious distress. I called the local vet and he said I could bring him right in. We encouraged each other that this must be some fluke accident and that in time, Isaac would be just fine. When we got to the vet's, he asked all the appropriate questions about him and took x-rays of his front legs and did some other tests. Soon he came in with the bad news, Isaac had some rare cancer/growth hormone problem and it caused him to grow quicker than his bones could develop. Then came the shocker, he couldn't just set his broken legs and expect that all would be fine. There simply wasn't any cure for him. He would have to be put to sleep. We were devastated. Our handsome dog would not be healed, divinely or otherwise.

Death, grief and loss are hard to understand and accept. Many of us pray for divine intervention into our lives, but we don't always seem to receive it. My experience tells me that we all have faced or may have to face times when someone or some pet we love is found to have a terminal illness or be involved in some accident or tragedy. At these times, we might question God and wonder where He is. Why doesn't God hear our prayers? We have prayed; we have believed; we have claimed our miracle in every religious way possible...but still we've lost our beloved. Why doesn't God spare the life of our father, mother, husband, wife, sister, brother, aunt, uncle, friend or pet? Why does God allow our relationships, our job, our business, our church to fail? Why? Why? Why?

Now, after thirty years, I could name so many other instances that were far more important to me than God saving the life of our dog. These were situations when I prayed for, greatly needed, and fully expected God to act favorably on my behalf. Sometimes I received the miracles that I prayed for, but it is not those times I question. It is when I didn't see the miracles for which my questions still remain. Is it possible that this life is just random and God doesn't really care to be involved or to intervene? Does whatever happen, just happen? Do our prayers really matter to God at all? Does He just do whatever He wants to do? Wouldn't God get more positive press if He always healed?

I have more questions than answers but I still take great consolation in the truth that the God I know and love is a God of love, compassion, power and healing. Even though I've struggled with these and many other sad situations, I rest assured that God never intended for us to have to feel all these pains. His plan for us was to enjoy a world without sin. Yet sin entered the world when Adam and Eve were deceived by the enemy of our souls. We continue the pattern. We now live in a fallen world. That's not God's fault; that's ours. Satan is responsible for all the evil, pain, disillusionment, grief and loss that we see in our world today. All of us must take personal responsibility for our own sins and shortcomings. We must never blame God for the tragedies of life. These were never part of His perfect plan for us. By accepting Jesus Christ as Lord and Savior, He has provided a way for us all who believe to live with Him in a place where sin, death, grief, and loss will never again enter. We will one day have all our questions answered. In the meantime, it's important to keep on praying, even if we don't always have every prayer answered in the way that we want it to be answered. Our miracle could be the next one!

Questions for today:

1) If God is the 'divine healer' and all powerful, why doesn't He heal all the time?

2) Whom do you blame for the bad things that happen in life?

3) Why do some of our prayers get answered and others don't?

Prayer: Dear Lord, help us to accept that your way is the best way! Help us to be people of faith who are willing to keep praying and believing for miracles! Help us to cope with and grow from the losses we experience. Amen.

Day#17
"Keep Me Safe 'Til the Storm Passes By"
by Chaplain (COL)-R Harold T. Carlson

—⚏—

Biblical Theme: God alone is our ultimate source of safety. In Him, we are safe and secure.

Scripture for today:

Matthew 7:24-27 "Therefore everyone who hears these words of Mine, and acts upon them, may be compared to the wise man, who built his house upon the rock. And the rain descended, and the floods came, and the winds blew, and burst against that house; and yet it did not fall, for it had been founded upon the rock. And everyone who hears these words of Mine, and does not act upon them, will be like a foolish man, who built his house upon the sand. And the rain descended, and the floods came, and the winds blew, and burst against that house; and it fell, and great was its fall."

There was no rain. It was the last week of January, 1975. Judy, Alida and I lived in a rural farm house just nine miles north of Pipestone, Minnesota. The green colored house had been a school at one time. It was a sort of box with winter entry leading down to the unfinished basement and upstairs to the main floor with the kitchen, living room and two bedrooms. My brother Bruce had come to pay us a visit. The tale he told was one that could have had a tragic ending, but God protected him. The winds had begun to blow. They were surging across the plains of southwestern Minnesota at 50-70 miles per hour. The snow was blowing and drifting. Visibility was nearly zero. He spoke of getting out of his car and walking to insure that he was on the road. He plowed on north and his 1974 Plymouth Scamp stayed, almost miraculously, on the road. Our driveway was just off of Highway 75. He pulled the car into the driveway and there it sat for almost ten days! The snow packed so tightly into the engine area that it was a solid block of snow from the grill to the back of the engine. The landscape began to change that day and a vigil of survival began.

Judy was full-term. We were expecting our second child. Bruce, my youngest brother Chuck and a nephew, Steve Eastep were at our house. While we were enjoying each other's company, the winter storm was setting in with fury and unrelenting resolve. Out on the road, not more than one hundred and fifty feet away, drifts of ten to fifteen feet of snow had come. The howling wind and the swirling of the snow surrounded our dwelling. The wind chill was thirty to sixty below zero. We were at the mercy of our furnace and the hope of keeping the electricity.

Would the baby come in this kind of a setting? Judy became restless and on the morning of the second day of the blizzard she decided that she simply must go out the back door and experience the wintry assault that enveloped us. I reluctantly walked with her to the back door. Then, I waited. I waited longer. She did not return. I began to call her. She could not see me and did not hear me. Such was the power of that horrendous winter day.

She began to walk in small circles. It was hard to walk because of the piles of snow. As she circled, she caught a glimpse of the house and then heard my loud cry sounding her name. I reached out and took her arm. She was safe. This was a very frightening experience. I loathe and am deathly afraid of blizzards and will always have that posture towards these killer storms.

On the third day, the storm abated. The sun came out; the snow stopped and we began to see the landscape. It was amazing. We could have been on a glacier. There was little that was familiar. Bruce's car was nearly covered. The highway was a small mountain of snow. Nothing mechanical moved. We were entrapped in a winter maze of mounded snow and ice.

All of us kept asking Judy, "Are you feeling any labor pains?" She was. They were 'Bracken-Hicks' as I recall. We thought our only course of action would be experiencing a home birth. I had taken a few LaMaze classes. But, I was not prepared to deliver our second child. Around noon, a neighbor came to us on a snowmobile. I was the teacher and basketball coach of the second smallest high school in Minnesota. Its name was Verdi...just south of Lake Benton. The neighbors said they were concerned about us as they knew Judy was very pregnant. We thanked them and told them that we were okay but concerned about getting to town, should we need to go. They invited us to call them if they could be of help.

By the grace of God, who kept us safe from the storm, Elnora Lee (our light meadow dweller...Elnora-meadow... Lee-light) did not arrive until the 6th of February. The roads had been cleared so that they were passable. We had chiseled some ice from Bruce's engine and heated the rest so that it melted. Our guests were able to leave. There we were, waiting for our little girl's arrival.

That is my most poignant memory of our rural route dwelling near Pipestone, Minnesota. Our ninth house had held firmly. The floods had not swamped it for there was no rain. The cold had not frozen it for God protected us with the continuity of our electrical power. The raging storm, blowing snow and howling winds had not frightened us beyond measure. We were kept safe by our loving, Heavenly Father.

After the storm, Elnora Lee was born. She came into the world in Pipestone, Minnesota. She is now thirty-two. Her husband is a LTC in the Marine Corps. She is a writer, poet, thinker, homemaker and lovely Christian woman. She has a heart that beats with mine. Her tender manner and endearing ways are treasures to me. Thank you, God, for keeping her safe within Judy's womb until the fullness of your timing for her birth. Thank you for keeping us safe 'til the storm passed by'.

Questions for today:

1) Have you ever had a ninth house? Do you have a story of God's protection that comes to your mind as you recall that dwelling or any other dwelling you've had?

2) Have you ever been in a blizzard or a raging storm? What kinds of thoughts do you recall from that experience?

3) Do the names of your children have special meaning? All six of ours do. If you haven't had children yet, consider naming them with designations that reflect significant meaning from scripture or from family affiliation.

4) Is your present house founded and grounded upon the 'Solid Rock', Jesus Christ our Lord? If not, why not invite Him into your heart and life right now? Without a doubt, the storms of life will come to you. They come to all of us. Let's choose now to be ready. Only Jesus can keep us safe 'til the storm passes by'. Only Jesus can be with us if the storm doesn't pass by and if we aren't safe when the ravages of the unexpected turbulences of life come our way.

Prayer: Dear Lord and Gracious Heavenly Father, Your protecting hand kept our little, growing family safe over thirty years ago. We could have died in that storm. As we recall your safeguarding of our lives, we think of the truth that You, and You alone, are our only source of ultimate safety. Thank you that Elnora Lee, our little child, yet unborn in that storm, has invited you into her life. Thank you for the powerful influence that your life in her is making upon her community in Quantico, Virginia. Thank you for her Godly husband and children: Hannah, Ethan, Lydia, Ian and baby Phillip. All of them know you. May each person who reads this devotional today pause to thank you for your protection. If they do not have you as their Savior, as the Lord who stands to forgive their sins and to heal their lives, may they open their hearts to You this day. In the strong, protecting and powerful name of Jesus Christ we pray, Amen.

Day #18
"Star, the Dog Who Ran with the Wrong Crowd"

by Charles J. Carlson

Biblical Theme: We need to think carefully about who we have close relationships with. Bad company, even our family, can help to create bad character and bad consequences.

Scripture for today:

Proverbs 16:15 "There is a way that seems right to a man but in the end it leads to death." Numbers 16 (the whole chapter, really) but specifically Numbers 16:28-33 "Then Moses said, "This is how you will know that the Lord has sent me to do all these things and that it was not my idea: If these men die a natural death and experience only what usually happens to men, then the Lord has not sent me. But if the Lord brings about something totally new, and the earth opens it mouth and swallows them, with everything that belongs to them, and they go down alive into the grave, then you will know that these men have treated the Lord with contempt. As soon as he finished saying all this, the ground under them split apart and the earth opened its mouth and swallowed them, with their households and all Korah's men and all their possessions. They went down alive into the grave, with everything they owned; the earth closed over them, and they perished and were gone from the community."

There is something magnetic about family. Either we are drawn to them or they repel us. It is rare that we are simply 'ambivalent'. I think that I came from an awesome family and extended family. I love my family and I am drawn to all of them, for different reasons. When I was young, I wanted to be like my older brother Tim. I admired him then especially for his athletic prowess and in time, for his choice of a life partner. So it was no surprise that I wanted to follow in his footsteps so much so that I found the future wife of my youth, when I was only 13. No, I didn't get married at 13, but I met Mary at their wedding. She is Judy's niece. We walked the aisle as candle lighters for their wedding back then and over time, we too fell in love. We eventually walked that very same church isle at our own wedding about seven years later.

For a time following, we lived only thirty miles from each other in South Dakota and it is there that this devotional story begins. They had acquired a beautiful Golden Retriever that they named Princess. Naturally wanting to be like them, when the time came for her to have puppies, we were elated. We and several other family members were given the opportunity to choose a pup for our very own. We chose a most handsome pup with a distinct star in the middle of his forehead, which he shortly outgrew. However, he didn't outgrow his name. He was and always will be a 'star' in the 'pet stable' in my mind.

Star went from puppyhood to full-grown by the time he was six months old. He was so inquisitive yet so obedient. He loved to explore the farm and especially the sprawling pasture that literally cut our farm in half. We had bought into the family farming operation and had moved from our first home at the Southeast South Dakota Experiment Farm to our own home and farm place. Star loved riding with me inside the cab of my purple 1964 GMC pickup and he was my constant companion. When he rode to town with me on farming errands, he made instant friends with whoever would give him a bit of attention. But farm work wasn't all that I thought about. I also liked to get away on vacation.

It is always a concern for a farmer when vacation time rolls around. Some farmers simply forego any vacations, opting instead to carefully watch over their livestock and crops. I was a firm believer and still am that vacations are important. I believe they take priority over making money. At the end of life, I doubt any of us will be happily remembering how we made that extra few hundred dollars back there 30-50 years ago. However, if we take some much needed vacation time, we and our family will have fond memories that they can cherish forever.

I was thrilled to know a young, but very responsible high schooler named Daryl. Daryl and I had become good friends during a very hard time in his life; a time when he lost his best friend to cancer at age 16. We worked with the youth group and Daryl frequently stopped by just to talk, laugh and sometimes cry with us. He had a heart of gold. Daryl was my perfect choice for someone to care for my fledgling farm as we planned to slip away for a week or so to visit family and refresh ourselves.

A few days before we were to leave on vacation, I got a call from my brother Tim. He and his family were also planning to be on vacation at about the same time. He asked if I would mind having Princess come down and stay on the farm with Star. This was an easy request to honor. They were family and the dogs were family. I explained that we too were going to be away but that I had a responsible person available to care for the animals. We agreed that since Princess was a 'city dog' that we should keep both of them locked up together for the week in one of the farm's chicken coops. The coop had a small fenced in area where the dogs could romp and play. Within a few days, both our families were happily off on vacation without a care in the world.

I'm sure you've heard the adage 'it is great to get away but there is no place like home'. I know that is how we felt as we approached our home that afternoon as scheduled. We were surprised to see Daryl's pickup in our farmyard as we pulled in the driveway. When we got out, Daryl came to us with tears in his eyes. Through the tears, he explained that the dogs had been just fine most all week long. He had even spent extra time petting and playing with them and they'd gotten along so well.

But unfortunately, just the day before, they had probably become restless with our absence and had dug a hole under the chicken wire fence and run free. Instead of running out to explore the pasture that Star loved to play in, the dogs chose to run down the ditch along the highway. They likely had a wonderful time that afternoon and were very proud of their new found freedom. Had they simply stayed along the fence by the cornfield just playing and chasing each other around as they loved to do, everything would have been fine. But for whatever reason, when they had gotten to the corner south of the farm place, Princess decided to dart across the road. The neighbor who struck and killed Star said that neither of the dogs seemed to see or hear his pickup coming at them or the sound of his horn or his brakes as he tried to avoid the inevitable. It seems that Princess, the loving caring mother had led her son into a very dangerous and deadly situation. Chores for Daryl that sad afternoon had included locking Princess securely inside the chicken coop and carefully, tearfully burying Star in the garden plot next to the road.

My point in bringing up this sad event isn't to place blame on ourselves, my brother, on Princess, Star, Daryl or the neighbor who killed our beloved pet. It seems that the first verse suggested for this devotional might just also apply in 'doggie' world too. There is a way that seems right, but it ends in death! I'm sure if Princess and Star had any clue about what awaited them outside that secure fence we'd left them in, they would have stopped digging and remained content until their owners returned. But they weren't content. In their world, they had once had it much better and they wanted to get back to that place. They longed for the freedom that 'other' life had given to them.

Such was the mindset of the people in the story that I recommended for your reading today. It was the story of the Israelites that followed after Korah and the other 250 well-known community leaders that became dissenters and opposed Moses and Aaron. I'm sure that these men felt strongly that what they were doing was right, but as you noticed, their way ended in death. Not only for them, but also for their families that followed their horrible advice by taking on their dissenting ways. They had felt that they had every right to complain about their lot in life. They longed for the way it used to be, and they wanted a way out of the desert experience that they thought was hemming them in and causing them distress. They thought they knew a better way than God's way. I'm sure that if Korah, his family and followers had known what awaited their contemptuous acts against God's anointed leaders, they would have quickly changed their minds. Truly, there is a way that seems right to us, but if it's not God's way, it will end in death. That death could be physical death, emotional death, financial death but most certainly and ultimately it will be spiritual death and separation from God. Yet we can be encouraged by the admonition from scripture (Romans 6:23) which states "the wages of sin is death, but the gift of God is eternal life through Jesus Christ our Lord." None of us needs to fear death; for we can choose life!

Questions for today:

1) What is your favorite vacation memory?

2) Are you a complainer? Do you always long for something you can't have or once had and lost?

3) With what crowd are you running? Is your friendship group or family group a positive or negative influence on your life?

4) Is there a particular way you are living your life right now that you know is wrong, but you aren't willing to change? If so, what keeps you from making the change you need to make?

Prayer: Dear Heavenly Father, help us to be content with the boundaries that you have set for us within your Holy Word. Please protect us from those who would want to deceive or ensnare us in situations that we know are wrong or could cause us 'death' or separation from you. Help us to be willing to change anything You ask us to change so that we might have a closer, more positive relationship with You. Amen.

Day#19
"What Was I Thinking?"
by Chaplain (COL)-R Harold T. Carlson

—ɱ—

Biblical Theme: Sound judgment and discernment are spiritual qualities but they are also practical attributes that we must nurture in our thoughts, actions and deeds.

Scripture for today:

Proverbs 3:21-24 "My son, preserve sound judgment and discernment, do not let them out of your sight; they will be life for you, an ornament to grace your neck. Then you will go on your way in safety, and your foot will not stumble; when you lie down, you will not be afraid; when you lie down, your sleep will be sweet."

It was a delightfully beautiful two-story, colonial bungalow. This was our second, purchased home. The blizzard experience of 1975 was a strong motivator for our moving nine miles further from my job and into the city of Pipestone, Minnesota. Here, we were literally on the block of the hospital. The street had nice sidewalks, mature trees, well-kept lawns and a most inviting environment for any family, young or old. From the perspective of a dwelling, this place could easily have been a house in which our family grew and stayed for decades. That, for us, did not happen.

The upstairs bedroom had some unusual wallpaper. I think ducks, animals, blues, whites and reds were predominant. I didn't mind it. Changing the walls meant spending money and I would have preferred just living with it. But, I did promise Judy that we could change the décor. So, one day as I went upstairs, much to my consternation and surprise, a piece of the wallpaper had been lifted, ripped and torn away. I was furious! When I showed this to Judy, her response was simply, "You said we could replace it so I wanted to get a little head start." I glared at her and actually pulled her hair. Then, she pulled mine. I deserved more. What a way for a young Christian couple to act! In spite of ourselves, and really in spite of myself, we began some positive resolution regarding this matter. The positive outcome dollar-wise was unexpected and not far away.

I had some old tires out by our single garage. The structure, along with our home, was frame construction. Well-built and attractive are descriptors that linger as I recall this abode. In the living room, with solid oak floors, was a nice fireplace with an attractive mantle. One night, while Judy and the girls were away, I decided to build a fire and burn one of the tires. I have rarely done something more foolish. It started somewhat easily and then, almost too soon to imagine, black smoke began to rush into our living room. I called 911 and very soon they were there. The firemen came to a house that now had black smoke coming out of the closed front door. Quickly, they put a ladder up and broke the upstairs window of the room that now needed new wallpaper. I didn't like this at all, but it was effective and they rapidly extinguished the fire. Considerable smoke damage had occurred.

Judy came home. She was aghast and appalled. Her response was shared by many in the small town. The newspapers had a small story about the fire and its cause. At the grocery store she heard others talking about the 'idiot' who tried to burn a tire in his fireplace. Being the lovely, loyal wife that she was, she refused to acknowledge that the culprit was indeed, her husband. But, my lack of sound judgment and discernment were not a total loss to our family of four. We had a friend in the Twin Cities, some two hundred plus miles away who had just begun a Service Master Business. He somewhat reluctantly came to do a thorough cleaning. We gleaned @$850.00 from the insurance and his charge was @$500.00. With the balance, we got new wallpaper and yes; we gave to the girls' room with the reds, blues, whites, ducks and animals a more feminine and appealing look.

Before the tire incident, my sleep had been quite good, unless I had awakened to think of our room with the ripped wallpaper that now needed repair or my reactions to it. Paradoxically, after the fire, we repapered the room. God transformed that place of conflict and debate into one of tranquility for our family. God used this series of events to begin a process of my growing up and tuning myself to better thinking and deeper insight. I truly was moved to a place where my sleep, for the entire night, could be sweet.

It is hard to remember this idyllic dwelling without remembering the tire fire. After less than a year, we left that place. God was calling us to seminary and life in the United States Army as an Army Chaplain.

Questions for today:

1) A tenth home...have you had one?

2) What is the dumbest thing you ever did in this home or in any of your houses?

3) What is the most dynamic conflict you and your spouse have ever had? Were your children involved? How did God help to bring positive resolution or was there no resolution?

4) What advice do you have for young couples who want to redecorate their homes?

5) Can you define and give examples of the qualities of sound judgment and discernment?

Prayer: Dear loving, Heavenly Father, I am sorry that I got so mad at Judy nearly thirty years ago. Help me only to make promises that I intend to keep and help me to allow You to temper my temper and my emotions. Thank you for the positive memories of our home in Pipestone, Minnesota. Thank you also for firemen. They are such lifesavers and rescuers of the wise and the foolish. Thank you for Jesus Christ. He is our Redeemer and Friend. He is truly the giver of sound judgment and discernment. Help me and my family to incline ourselves to your thoughts and ways so that what we do physically, emotionally and spiritually is laced with the gifts of sound judgment and discernment. In Your Holy name we pray, Amen.

Day #20
"Elijah, Here Today...Gone Today!!"
by Charles J. Carlson

—ᴍ—

Biblical Theme: Each day we have is a gift from God. Use it wisely.

Scripture for today:
Ps. 118:24 "This is the day the Lord has made; let us rejoice and be glad in it. Ps. 39:4 Show me, O Lord, my life's end and the number of my days; let me know how fleeting is my life."

Job 14: 1-2, 5 "Man is of few days and full of trouble. He springs up like a flower and withers away; like a fleeting shadow, he does not endure. "Man's days are determined; you have decreed the number of his months and have set limits he cannot exceed."

Ps. 139:16 "Your eyes saw my unformed body. All the days ordained for me were written in your book before one of them came to be."

Matt. 6:19-20 "Do not store up for yourselves treasures on earth, where moth and rust destroy, and where thieves break in and steal. But store up for yourselves treasures in heaven, where moth and rust do not destroy, and where thieves do not break in and steal. For where your treasure is, there your heart will be also."

This is perhaps my most embarrassing and hard to fathom 'dog story'. In fact, it will take longer for me to type this devotional about Elijah than the amount of time that I owned him. In the Old Testament in 2 Kings 2:11-12, you can read about one of God's main prophets named Elijah. It was after years of effective ministry that God whisked him away in a whirlwind. Unfortunately, that's not what happened to my dog, Elijah.

In order to fully understand Elijah's story, you'll need a little background. Elijah was one of several litter mates to Star, our beautiful Golden Retriever that I told you about previously. Elijah was one of the few pups that didn't make it into the hands of a relative. Instead, Elijah had been sold to a pastor acquaintance of my brother. Paul Cohen and his wife, Marcia, lived at the Komstad Covenant Church parsonage, which was right across the busy highway from the Southeast South Dakota Experiment Farm. The farm was the first place that I worked full-time as a married adult. Incidently, I too became the pastor at Komstad Covenant Church about ten years later while attending seminary at the North American Baptist Seminary in Sioux Falls, South Dakota.

While working at the Experiment Farm, I would frequently stop after work to shoot basketball hoops with Paul and compare dog stories. Naturally, when Star was killed, Paul too was sad for us. He loved his dog, Elijah, but he wasn't entirely happy with him. Paul had been working incessantly to make Elijah a hunter, but Elijah just didn't seem to get it. I didn't think Elijah was as stunning a specimen as our 'Star' was but nonetheless he was a great dog. His markings were a much deeper, darker red color than the golden, blonde-haired dog we had loved.

One day while we were shooting hoops, Paul made the off-handed comment that he wished that he could find an adult Golden that already knew all about hunting and if he did, he'd gladly sell Elijah to us. He didn't know it but I took that as a personal challenge. Surely somebody would have a dog that fit that category and then we'd get the chance to be like other family members by getting to raise another one of Princess's pups.

For the next couple weeks I religiously scoured the ads in the local newspapers, gas stations, restaurants and banks.... basically any place that anyone would put up an ad. We spotted the ad in the newspaper and without too much fanfare, we became the 'proud owners' of an adult Golden named Shadrach, who could indeed hunt and retrieve. Shadrach was a beautiful animal, but he had a couple of peculiarities. First off, someone had cut off his tail as a pup. I didn't find that look particularly attractive. Next, he had an annoying habit of trying to use people's legs as practice for mating season. Other than that, hey...he was very well-behaved.

The next day, after work, I stopped by the pastor's house and told him of my find. I explained all that I knew about Shadrach and asked Paul if he'd really like to exchange dogs. He did, especially right then, because only a couple of days before, Elijah had gotten off his chain and run out onto the busy highway. Paul and Marcia had visions of a very unhappy ending for their pet and they really wanted one that was content to stay at home in the yard without a chain. We agreed to an even exchange and Shadrach was soon their dog. I couldn't have been more thrilled.

The following morning, Shadrach made the trip with me to work. He and Elijah seemed to get along well and I picked up my new dog after work. Because I had been a frequent visitor at the parsonage, Elijah had no trouble going with me in my pickup truck. This particular day had gone overtime for me and I was in a hurry to get home before dark so I could do my own chores. Having had to stop for this dog exchange didn't help my timeline any. As we traveled the seventeen mile trip home, we bonded. Elijah had some great qualities and he looked so stately sitting right next to me on the seat of my truck. He couldn't seem to decide if he liked viewing the road as we flew along or if he just liked lying down on the seat and putting his head in my lap.

The sun had all but gone down by the time we got home. No one else was home that evening but me. I remember that I tied a rope securely to his collar and then tied the rope to the steel railing of the front porch stoop. I wanted to play some more with him and feed him before I put him away in the barn overnight. Our yard was right next to a fairly busy highway. I remember thinking about how glad I was that we had put up a chain link fence all around the yard. I didn't have a care in the world as I left Elijah for just a few minutes so that I could start my tractor and begin using the tractor and loader to scoop silage from the silage pile into the cattle's feed bunks. As I labored with my tractor, I was replaying all the amazing events that led up to us having this new pet. I knew that both Elijah and I were lucky to have each other. Well….maybe not!

It was getting hard to see and I wished I had lights on my equipment. I had only taken a load or two of silage with the loader to the feed bunk when I heard the terrible noise of backing over something 'alive'. I didn't have a moment's notice. I hadn't seen or heard anything. I figured one of my pigs had gotten out. I quickly stopped and looked down at the ground. I was shocked to see that my victim was not a pig; it was Elijah! Truthfully a dog is no match for the large rear wheels of a tractor and loader. Evidently he had either broken or chewed through the rope that I had tied him up with. He must have been drawn to the noise of the tractor, the sound of the livestock, or maybe he just wanted to be by me again. For whatever reason, he jumped the chain link fence while the cattle were getting their supper and he never even got the opportunity for a 'last supper'. In a flash, my near perfect day turned to disaster. My lovely, lively new pet that had been in my possession for less than half an hour was dead and I was devastated.

Some things in life are just not explainable. My questions came fast and furious. How could any one person have so much bad luck with pets? Come to think of it, it wasn't just pets that didn't seem to fair well for me. I had already experienced many more of life's trials than a man of my age needed to endure. The truth is, some of life's hardest trials don't just surround the untimely deaths or accidental deaths of our pets. Many of the most difficult trials involve family, friends, acquaintances or co-workers. We just don't know what a day might hold. We just can't adequately prepare for some of the things that happen to us. Therefore, we should never take our life, or the life of someone or something we love for granted. We need to embrace each day that we are given, see it as a blessing from God and live it to the fullest. I remember my mom used to say something like "much too soon this life is past, only what's done for Christ will last".

Our scripture readings for today admonished us to realize the brevity of life and make the most of it. Keep in mind that just because God knows the number of our days and knows that we too will one day face death, he isn't the cause of our death or the cause of the grief that we endure because those we love have had to see tragedy or untimely deaths.

How can we make the most of every day? The secret is in recognizing our life as a gift that can and should be enjoyed. "This is the day that the Lord has made, let's rejoice together and be glad in it"!

Questions for today:

1) Have you ever lost a pet to death? Do you still think about that pet?

2) Have you even been 'responsible' for the untimely death of a pet? How did that make you feel? What did you do to recover from those bad feelings? Have you forgiven yourself?

3) When a pet or a loved one dies, whom do you blame? Do you think God is responsible?

4) Are you blaming God for not loving you or your family member enough to heal you or a family member when you or a family member needed healing or sparing from some tragedy?

5) How can we store up 'treasures in heaven'?

Prayer: Dear Heavenly Father, thank you for this new day that you have given to us. We don't know what this day might hold but we look forward to it and chose to be happy in it. We pray for your protection, guidance and strength to accomplish something positive for You and your kingdom today. Please help us to forgive you, if we are blaming you for the bad things that happen to us. Help us to forgive ourselves, if we need to do so. Help us to recover from the pain of the untimely, unexpected and unfortunate experiences of death which we have had in this life, not only with the people that we love, but also with the pets that we have had in our care. In Your precious and Holy Name we pray, Amen.

Day#21
"But Godliness, With Contentment, Is Great Gain"

by Chaplain (COL)-R Harold T. Carlson

—ᚥ—

Biblical Theme: God wants us, his children, to learn to be content with what we have.

Scripture for today:
I Timothy 6:6 "But Godliness, with contentment, is great gain".

We sold our white, colonial home in Pipestone, Minnesota. It was hard to let it go. In reality, we should have let it go sooner. We had a good offer, almost one-third more than we had given for it less than a year earlier. But, I thought we could get more. Not only did we not get that extra money, we hired a realtor to sell the home for us. God had called us to seminary and we needed the money.

On the outside, 1906 South Duluth, in Sioux Falls, South Dakota was modest at best. The house looked small. Really, it wasn't. Almost all that one could imagine had been done to maximize space in this place. The basement was finished. The rooms were well-kept and the bathrooms had new fixtures and looked very good. Only the kitchen roof was somewhat swayed but had no leaks.

God had given to us a new home less than ten blocks from North American Baptist Seminary. We had a small nest egg; we had the G. I. Bill of $474 per month for education and our house payment was @ $200.00. Why was it that we stayed in this home only one year?

I have been, and still am at times, opportunistic and somewhat impulsive. Starting my second year of seminary, my Middler year, I thought that another sale of a home would net us needed cash. That was kind of true. What I didn't factor in was that the escalating real estate market was burning out quickly. Neither did I calculate the cost of another place that needed repairs. Our present home had needed nothing really.

You guessed it. We sold our place. Yes, we did realize some profit. But, we bought a troubled dwelling. Fast money in homes was over. Now, as I began this year of seminary and continued into the last one, we not only had a different house with a higher house payment but we also had the costs of a new roof, new brick work on the front steps and inside paint work. Even with these improvements, this home looked a lot better than it actually was.

It was December 8, 1977. Judy was pregnant. We had $400 in insurance for the birth of our child. It was nearly 70 degree below zero with the wind chill. Labor pains had begun. We had toyed with the idea of a 'home birth' but I was not prepared for that. On top of that, we had serious plumbing problems. We were getting water in our unfinished basement. On this bleak day, workers were tunneling and 'torpedoing' a hole from the street to our waterline. I would intermittently check on Judy. Her labor increased. A friend came over in the later afternoon and said, "Judy, you have to get the hospital."

Sioux Valley Hospital was only five blocks distant. Our dog, a Golden Retriever, came and licked Judy's arm. I came in and decided that Kathy was right. Off we went. This day lives in memory.

From the time we entered the hospital door to the time that Judy delivered Elizabeth Christine Carlson was seven minutes. The birth began in the labor room and we never made it to delivery. There was no doctor. The intern was almost in shock. Our new baby lay in the birth canal, almost born in blood. Finally, the student doctor took her out and patted her back. She gave a cry and all seemed well. It wasn't. Apparently a lack of oxygen left our daughter with multiple special needs. That was over twenty-nine years ago.

Why do things, like this, happen to God's children? Would a more normal birth have occurred had we stayed at 1906 South Duluth? Was a lack of contentment part of the reason I had not tuned sooner to Judy's condition or was the concern about money the motivator for our delayed journey to the hospital? These remain unanswered questions.

Elizabeth is a gem. She is a blessing to us, to all whom we meet and especially, to children. She will never be normal. She reads, walks, swims, laughs, plays games and interacts with relative ease. Her speech is different but she is understandable. But she is, and will always be, our special child.

Our home at 1326 West 15th was the place where 'Liz' learned to walk. Since she never crawled normally, walking was a great challenge. When she caught herself, it was more often with her head than her hands. We tried to keep her away from sharp objects. She was determined to walk and she did. That determination has kept her motivated. Even as I write this devotional, she is having a 'home schooling' lesson from her wonderful mother.

But, when I allow myself to muse; and I don't do this often, I wonder. What would our third child's life be like had I been more content? Would it have made any difference at all? Really, I'll never know. But I do know that learning to be content with what we have is part of God's heartbeat for all of us, his dear children. Thank you, God, for Elizabeth. I love her and I am learning from her. May her life always remind me to think about what your desire for us really is.

May you, in your kindness, keep us young so that we can care for her and give to her the love and home that she needs as she matures.

Questions for today:

1) Have you ever had an eleventh home? Describe it. Do you live in it now?

2) What is the coldest it has ever been in any of the homes in which you have lived?

3) What is the worst repair that you can remember which any of your homes required?

4) Have you ever had a special needs child? What are some of the lessons that this child, of any age, has taught and is teaching to you and to your family?

Prayer: Dear God, Thank you for your gracious love to our family. We will never understand the whys of December 8, 1977. But Lord, we trust you. The gift of Elizabeth Christine has been one of wonder, insights into your tender heart and also some times of being stretched beyond measure as we yearn for wholeness in this family member whom we dearly love. Build into us a content-ment that finds your love and your ways the only ones for which we yearn. Make us cautious to make impulsive decisions that could easily change our lives for the worse for an entire lifetime. Give to us your peace to accept what we cannot change and trust you for what lies ahead. In the name of the powerful Lord, Who will make all things new and all things right, Amen.

Day #22
"Champ...Struck Down and Left for Dead"

by Charles J. Carlson

—ᴎᴎ—

Biblical Theme: God is the Divine Healer, both for people and for animals!

Scripture for today:

Ecc. 3:1,3,7 "There is a time for everything; a time to kill and a time to heal; a time to tear and a time to mend."

Ps. 107:19-22 "Then they cried to the Lord in their trouble, and he saved them from their distress. He sent forth his Word and healed them; he rescued them from the grave. Let them give thanks to the Lord for his unfailing love and his wonderful deeds."

Matt. 7:11 "If you, then, though you are evil, know how to give good gifts to your children, how much more will your Father in heaven give good gifts to those who ask him!"

By now you have realized that our family hasn't had spectacular luck with our dogs but thankfully, the story of Champ will be an exception. We got Champ as a beautiful puppy from extended family in Minnesota. From day one he instantly bonded with us, our son Chad and his little sister,

Kirsten. They loved helping me do chores on the farm but they especially liked exploring the grove, the pasture, the outbuildings, their tree house and the entire farmyard. I have limitless memories of our happy days there.

When Champ came to live with us, he soon learned all about his boundaries; including where he could go and what he was allowed to do. He was very obedient and rarely pressed his limits. I'm sure it was an adjustment for him when Chad started school. Our farm home was located very close to the highway. Chad's bus driver for kindergarten was just a great guy. Gordon Larson cared for each of those kids on his bus as if they were his very own. He arranged with us a special way to pick Chad up for school. Instead of stopping out on the highway, he'd pull that big yellow bus right into our driveway...let Chad safely board before he'd turn the bus around and head for town. We really appreciated his doing this. From Champ's earliest days on, he would greet Chad by the front porch, in the morning before school, and walk or run with him in the driveway until the bus came to pick him up.

By the time first grade came around, the bus routes had been changed and we had a new bus driver. This driver felt Chad was old enough to cross the highway to catch the bus in the same way other kids did. He was right and Chad quickly adapted. Champ, however didn't seem to feel the same way. He had to learn that he couldn't cross the road with Chad. He learned that he must be content to just sit at the end of the driveway and watch him from there. It took us a few days to help Champ learn his boundaries but after that it went off without a hitch.

One morning, however, the bus was running late. The dog had been patient for some time. He sat there at the end of the driveway just watching his buddy as he stood by the mailbox across the road of our sometimes busy highway. When he seemingly couldn't take it any longer, he ran across the road and stood there beside Chad. As his protector, it looked pretty harmless. But I really didn't want Champ getting used to crossing the road. So I stepped away from the large living room windows and went out on the front porch. I called for Champ to come home. He didn't. It was windy and I thought he didn't hear me. So I called again but still he didn't come. This kind of annoyed me and I quickly stepped back into the house to grab my boots. I put them on as fast as I could, stepped back on the porch and called him again. Unfortunately for all of us, I hadn't looked very carefully down the road or I would have noticed that a pickup was barreling up the road towards our farm place. I started up the driveway and then, at the worst possible moment, Champ decided to become obedient. He left his post and sped across the road. Tragically, he didn't make it! That pickup, with horn blowing hit him hard, and the driver didn't slow down. I knew he was a 'goner'. I quickly ran across the driveway and scooped up my terrified son in my arms. I glanced at Champ as he lay motionless there on the highway. I could see blood. I would have to deal with him later; but for now Chad needed me most. This would be one of his first experiences with dealing with the death of a pet.

By the time I got back to the house, Mary was standing on the porch with the front door open. We both comforted Chad as best we could. We brought him into the living room, took off his coat and just kept hugging him and drying his eyes. I don't remember if he suggested it or if Mary or I did, but one of us said that we should pray for Champ. Mary and I knew all too well about the pains of losing pets and we hated that we were now losing another one. We stopped right then and there and we all began to pray, especially Chad. We asked God for strength to comfort us during this sad time. Chad was more direct. He wanted God to heal his pet so we joined in those prayers too. But truthfully, this was more for his benefit than for Champ's. Sure, we wanted God to

143

miraculously spare the dog's life but I don't think we really believed our prayers would accomplish anything. Neither of us had even looked out at Champ again for we were just concerned about our son. So after we prayed, we all bravely peeked out of the living room windows and to our amazement, Champ was alive...to a degree. Have you ever seen an animal do the death kick, with all four legs flailing as they lie helpless on the ground? It isn't a pleasant sight. Mary covered Chad's eyes and turned him away from the window. She got an old sheet for me and I went back outside to pick up Champ and put him out of his misery.

When I reached him he was leaning awkwardly on one hip and going round and round in circles in the middle of the highway. We had heard the bus go by and since then a few other cars. No one had stopped to help him. There was blood coming from his mouth. He was making ear piercing cries and his eyes showed his pain and fear. I spoke calmly to him and carefully laid him in the sheet. I had already envisioned taking him behind the barn and putting him to permanent rest. But as I was carrying him back in our driveway, it occurred to me what a miracle it was that he was alive at all. When I saw him get hit by the speeding pickup, I had thought he was dead for sure. As I looked at his bruised body, I was surprised that I didn't see more blood, guts or a broken leg. Instead of taking him behind the barn, I took him to the back door of the house and laid him carefully on the entry way floor.

He had already calmed down so much and his cries were now just occasional whimpers. He even tried to lick me with his bloody mouth. I began to have hope. I left him there and went back inside to the living room. We comforted Chad but made him no promises. It seemed that God, the divine healer, was answering our prayers. I let him pet Champ for a moment. I don't remember if we took Chad to school that day or not. What I do remember is that within a day, Champ was standing up on his own power. Within two days, he was drinking water and eating soft foods. Within a week, he could hobble about and within a month, he was his old self. He always had a slight limp in his walk and a hitch in his run after that; but that didn't bother him or us. I still believe God performed a miracle for us. Champ, 'the victor' was true to his name. He loved life and he loved us. He had been down for the count but he wasn't out! He had been hit hard, almost to the point of death, but he came up victoriously! It was a memorable resurrection for him! Our family pet remained with us for some time.

There are a couple thoughts that I am reminded of when I think of Champ's story. The first is an observation, the second a biblical truth. First, my observation is that God has a special place in his heart for children's prayers and it seems their prayers of faith get some well-deserved attention. I can't prove that, but I've seen it happen. The second truth is that God, our Divine Healer, operates in miraculous ways we don't always understand. He gives good gifts to those who ask Him. He cares both for people and for animals. However, my goal in writing this devotional is to build your faith so that you and your family, or those within your circle of influence, will be encouraged to pray. Remember, God does indeed answer prayer and prayer does change things. So keep praying, keep believing, keep asking, keep seeing needs and don't stop until you get an answer. The effectual, fervent prayers of God's people can and do make a difference. Will you be a difference maker in the kingdom of God?

Questions for today:

1) Have you ever prayed for God to heal an animal? Did He answer your prayer? Have you ever prayed for God to heal a family member, friend or acquaintance? Did He answer your prayer?

2) Do you believe that God still performs miracles today? If not, why not? Can you tell others about a miracle that you have seen, witnessed or heard?

3) Do you know of someone who needs a miracle touch in their life/situation from God today? Will you pray for them right now?

Prayer: Dear Heavenly Father, we thank you and praise you that you are true to Your Word and that your Word tells us that you are our 'Divine Healer'. Help us never to become callous towards You nor to the work of prayer. Lord, we admit that sometimes, when we don't get our prayers answered in the way that we want, we give up on prayer and even on You. Help us to be willing to be consistent and persistent in our praying. Today we want to pray for your miracle touch in the lives and situations of _____. We relinquish our will and ask for yours to be done instead. We thank you in advance for your answers to our prayers. In the precious, Holy Name of Jesus, we pray...Amen!

Day #23
"He Protects the Way of His Faithful Ones"
by Chaplain (COL)-R Harold T. Carlson

—ɷ—

Biblical Theme: God is our Protector.

Scripture for Today:
Proverbs 2:7-8 "He holds victory in store for the upright, He is a shield to those whose walk is blameless, for he guards the course of the just and protects the way of the faithful ones."

So far, the outcome is a very good one. Today, as I write, our eldest son, Kristian Lael…(Christian of/or from God) is studying in Springfield, Missouri where he is a Junior at Assemblies of God Theological Seminary. We and others are very proud of this male firstborn and thankful for God's obvious hand in and on his life.

Twenty-five years ago K-Dog, as I often call him now, had a hair-flattening day. We lived in our first Army Quarters. The address was 2848B Monfore in Fort Lewis, Washington. The dwelling was quite small. We had @1,100 square feet and when Kristian came to us there at Madigan Army Hospital, our family had six members. We had been there nearly two years. He was a handful and a most fun child. The Jewish Chaplain's wife 'prophesied (sort of) that he would not only be friend but a buddy. That has proven most true.

As a slight digression, I'll illustrate this with an incident that took place in November of 1998, which was a most challenging time for us. We had left our farm home and were being sent to Washington D.C. where I was to be the first ever chaplain for the United States Army Corps of Engineers. I do not like cities. On my first day reporting for duty, Kristian came along with me to find the Pulaski Building, three blocks north of the Capitol, and to be my buddy as I went to meet the 3-star General, LTG Joe Ballard. God provided in miraculous ways for me in that assignment, which even included Kristian's being my guide into the city.

In 1982, we shared a common driveway with our neighbors. Our little street wound around and we were the second set of duplexes on the turn. Across the back fence was a railroad tracks and a road even closer. Often we would hear the 75th Army Rangers as they were beginning their six to fifteen mile run. Kristian was most curious and had an interest in everything and everyone. But this day in memory could have been a tragic one.

Vicky was our neighbor. She was sort of likeable and very boundary challenged. She would often pop into our kitchen and have the most disparaging words for the hospital and her perception of their less than stellar care, as she perceived it. She would be an inspiration to the free-spirit homemakers who value many things, but not necessarily order. After the dishes had piled two to three feet on their stove, either she or her husband Terry would decide it was time. Yes, they washed their dishes. They didn't just throw them away. That would truly be free-spirited.

On that near fateful day, Kristian was out in the yard playing. Vicky had a late 1970's Chevy Station Wagon. Many will wonder what that is? Being in a hurry, as she often seemed to be, she got into her car, put it into reverse and began backing out of the driveway. She thought she heard something and miraculously, she stopped. Wedged under her car, between the tires, was Kristian! He had grease on his face and was berating our neighbor as he adroitly could do using the best words and tones I have ever heard from someone of that age. I only heard of this event. I was at work as the chaplain for 1/67 ADA (Air Defense Artillery) on the North Fort.

Truly, God spared Kristian's life. Our only son, at that time, was nearly a dead one. It is hard for me to even recount this story but it reminds me of our text. God protects the way of his faithful ones. Kit's life is now consumed with ministry and ministry preparation. Each week he leads worship for up to 800 Soldiers in Training. He has preached to them. He has led missions trips to Romania and been part of a trip to Israel. He just hosted a retreat for Air Force Airmen at a nearby Christain Retreat House called "Standdown Summit". I could go on and on but God has, through his mercy and love, inclined the K-Dog to Himself. You may wonder why such a name? Kristian pegged me "The Kern-Dog" after my promotion to Colonel in December of 2000 so I decided to pass a portion of my name on to him.

I do not know the ways that our son's life will take. Currently he is preparing for ministry as a Navy Chaplain. He loves the sea, literature, learning, international issues, persons of Islam who need Jesus and so many other things. While our paths cross less frequently than when he would stand by my side in our 1979 Chevy Station Wagon and share the sights of the road, my heart still travels with him. It also journeys with our other son Nels, who just began seminary yesterday and our other grown children, dearly loved and all in love with Jesus, our Lord.

Questions for today:

1) Have you ever lived in twelve places? Describe that last one.

2) Have you ever had a child nearly killed? What happened? How do you feel about this child?

3) Who is the most challenging neighbor you have ever had? Have you kept in touch? Are they still your neighbor?

4) Recount some events that demonstrate God's protection of you and your family.

Prayer: Dear Lord, Thank you for keeping Ensign Kristian Lael Carlson safe over twenty-five years ago. Today, as he commutes back to our home, some seventy-five miles away in a driving snowstorm, continue to be with him. Help all of our children to seek to make you the Lord and Protector of their lives. We know that some of our offspring may not be walking with You. In fact, some have never invited You into their lives. May they humble themselves even now and begin the most delightful and adventurous journey known to mankind, the journey with Jesus. In your most Holy Name we pray, Amen.

Day #24
"Cocoa, A Dog Without Boundaries"
by Charles J. Carlson

—w—

Biblical Theme: Bad things can happen when we don't learn to respect the boundaries we are given. Temptations come to all of us; but we can resist them.

Scripture for today:
Matt 26:41 "Watch and pray so that you will not fall into temptation. The spirit is willing, but the flesh is weak."

James 1:13-14 "When tempted, no one should say, "God is tempting me". For God cannot be tempted by evil, nor does he tempt anyone; but each one is tempted when, by his own evil desire, he is dragged away and enticed. Then, after desire has conceived, it gives birth to sin; and sin when it is full-grown, gives birth to death."

I Cor. 10: 12-13 "So, if you think you are standing firm, be careful that you don't fall! No temptation has seized you except what is common to man. And God is faithful; he will not let you be tempted beyond what you can bear. But when you are tempted, he will also provide a way out so that you can stand up under it."

From the moment we got Cocoa, our Cheasapeake Bay Retriever pup, from our next door neighbor, I knew we had our hands full. She was gorgeous and fun-loving but she was into everything, all the time, right from the start.

Her early teething stages of puppyhood probably drove her crazy; I know it almost did me in. She chewed up everything in sight. She could mess up her pen or the fenced in yard so quickly. It frequently looked like a tornado had come through or a bomb had gone off. It's not that she was a terribly bad dog; she just didn't get the need for boundaries and she couldn't resist temptation.

If you said 'no', she proceeded anyway. If you wanted her to retrieve, she wouldn't. If you finally got her to go pick up something, she wouldn't drop it out of her mouth when you asked her to. She basically wanted to do her own thing. She just wanted to live her life and she didn't want to have to answer to anyone. To say she was rebellious would be letting her off easily. Yet Cocoa was lovable and affectionate; she had our hearts.

As she got older she mellowed, but her curiosity didn't. Her downfall was the temptation that frequently took her way past the boundaries of her safe, secure farm life. What tempted her most was movement, particularly from tires or wheels. As a puppy, she had been famous for grabbing tricycle, bicycle or big wheel tires as our kids tried to ride on the sidewalk or in the driveway. When she was successful, she'd bite those tires so hard and shake her head like she was in a fierce battle and needed to conquer them. At first, it was fun to watch but in time; it became annoying. We did our best to nip her bad behavior in the bud.

Each time we disciplined her, she just didn't seem to understand why or what the big deal was. We set appropriate boundaries for her, yet inevitably she'd cross them. She didn't stop with the kids toys. As an adult dog, she would bark loudly and run full steam in an attempt to bite my car, pickup or tractor tires. When visitors came, she was in prime form and must have felt that she was personally responsible for saving the family from some grave danger. Truthfully, moving things annoyed her; they tempted her and she'd do anything necessary, including crossing her boundaries, to get at them.

I knew this couldn't go on like this forever. We needed to get her under control but I just wasn't sure how we would. I had heard of people who had cured their dogs of this bad habit by putting an old rag inside the hubcap of their car tire. They'd let a small portion of the rag hang out. Then they'd drive real slowly and when their dog bit the rag, they'd get flipped in the process...learn their lesson...and likely not attack wheels again. I was tempted but it seemed like a drastic approach and I didn't have the heart to try it. I knew with my luck, I'd kill her! I didn't want to be responsible for any more dog deaths.

One Sunday while we were at church, Cocoa did the ultimate in boundary breaking. She either jumped the fence or climbed under it. I don't know how she spent the morning, but I do know what her last boundary bursting act was. When we came home from church, as we were coming closer to our farm, we noticed that the highway showed the trauma of an animal having lost its life. On the pavement every few yards, there was a mixture of blood and body parts. As we neared home, everyone suddenly recognized that what we were seeing was what was left of our beloved Cocoa. I've never forgotten this scene and what it took to retrieve her for a proper burial.

Early that afternoon, we got a phone call. One of my high school friends was calling to explain what happened. Evidently Cocoa had decided to attack the huge fertilizer truck that was spreading fertilizer on the neighbor's field. The truck had those gigantic rubber tires that balloon out and stand well over six feet tall. Brad said she attacked the moving truck with a vengeance. When she missed the front tire, she tried for the back one and was squashed under the wheel and carried with the truck down the road. There would be no more boundary breaking temptations for Cocoa. She just never learned to resist the temptations that became her demise. It's too bad dogs aren't given the same Biblical promises that people are!

The scriptures for today tell us about temptation and that we don't have to give in to them. We can, in fact, be victorious over them. We don't have to cross boundaries into areas of sin that we know would not be good for us. As believers in Jesus Christ, the Holy Spirit will help to show us practical, accomplishable ways to escape. We are all tempted to cross boundaries that we shouldn't cross; but we don't have to give in to those temptations. God will help us, if we ask him.

Questions for today:

1) What are some boundaries that the Bible addresses?

2) Does your family have some boundaries that aren't to be crossed?

3) When is the last time you were tempted? What tempted you?

4) Did you give in to the temptation or did you see the way to escape it?

Prayer: Dear Heavenly Father, Forgive us for the times that we have crossed boundaries that shouldn't have been crossed and have given into temptations that we knew were wrong. Please help us to be stronger. Lord, we understand that resisting temptation won't always be easy. Help us to be watching for problem areas in our lives. Help us not to be too proud to pray for the help we need to resist temptation. We want to be victorious in our lives. In Jesus' name we pray, Amen.

Day #25
"Even the Sparrow Has Found a Home"
by (COL)-R Harold T. Carlson

—ᏁᎥ—

Biblical Theme: God helps us to find shelter and a place to live.

Scripture for today:
Psalms 84:1-3 "How lovely is your dwelling place, O Lord Almighty! My soul yearns, even faints, for the courts of the Lord; my heart and my flesh cry out for the living God. Even the sparrow has found a home, and the swallow a nest where she may have her young...a place near your altar, O Lord Almighty, my King and my God."

We felt absolutely vulnerable. Our family of seven had towed a 1966, twenty foot Terry trailer from Fort Lewis, Washington to Washington, D.C. This was an epic journey for our older vehicle, a Suburban. It was also our thirty square feet of floor space mobile home. A fellow officer, Nelson Ard, had driven our 1978 Dodge Diplomat Wagon from the west coast to the east coast as he was leaving the Army and going to Portsmouth, Virginia. PCSing is what we call it in the military. That stands for a permanent change of station. Our 1971 'Suburb' did its job and did it well. The wind deflector more than paid for its purchase price. Our anticipation of life in, or near the Capitol, was high.

Just prior to our trip to D.C, we spent a few weeks vacationing with family members in the Midwest. Then, we made the final launch to the Capitol. Bottom line: there was no available housing offered to us by the Walter Reed Army Medical Center's Housing Office. Rent was very high and a family of our size was difficult to accommodate. So...we began a sojourn, a vigil, in Greenbelt Park. It was summer and very hot. We ran an extension cord from the park bathrooms to our little trailer so that we could have a fan running at night. This was our link to some mild comfort. But, the Park Rangers weren't too happy and reprimanded us repeatedly for this 'transgression'. The outlook for a home at this new assignment was bleak. But then, it happened.

We were searching for something to rent and we ran across 1636 Brisbane in Silver Spring, Maryland. It was a nice area, rather quiet and near Walter Reed and to the schools. The corner lot was overgrown and looked somewhat haunted. It had been a rental for many years and no one seemed to demonstrate ownership of the place. All of this, to include the requirement of two additional months of rent as a damage deposit, did not deter us from closing the rental deal. This place transitioned us from the world of the homeless to the world of those who had found a home.

The misery of warm nights, small quarters and an aimlessness and fear of finding no place to dwell were over. We had certainly bonded as a family but this new place was just what we needed. The whole neighborhood came over in the first few weeks. Why? We began to cut back the overgrown shrubs, mow the grass and treat the place as if it were our own.

As I sit here overlooking one of our valleys today, homelessness is far away. However, we have been having a siege of cold, snowy weather in Missouri. It is really atypical for our parts. Oh, we have a snow here, a snow there, three or four days of cold but then...the sun returns and temperatures in the fifties often interrupt winter. While we sit in our large kitchen overlooking two converging valleys, we are literally swamped with hungry birds. Judy loves to feed and watch the birds. As I watch them, I think of our scripture today, "Even the sparrow hath found her a house, and the swallow a nest, where she may lay her young; even thine altar, O Lord of Hosts, my King and my God." That translation is the King James Version. Its words are so comforting because they invite me to remember that our Creator, who watches over the birds, is the same Lord who watches over us, his children.

As houses go, 1636 Brisbane, was in the lower half of the places that we have lived. But, from the perspective of God's keeping his promises to us to care for us and to help us to find a roof over our heads; the place was as important to our family as if it had been a palace. Coupled with our text, I am reminded of Jesus' words in the Gospels, "Consider the lilies of the field; they toil not, neither do they spin. Yet Solomon in all of his glory was not arrayed like one of these. How much more will He care for you, oh ye of little faith?" Yes, God had cared for us. We were not forgotten. We too had found a home.

I had some faithless moments in Greenbelt Park, Maryland almost twenty-four years ago. I felt that God's care for me and our young family was very far away. The nights were miserably long and morning only brought more torpid, uncertain living but...God was faithful. He helped us to find a home and to build lingering memories. Truly, this home was a Godsend. Thankfully, it was also quite a short sojourn. Amazingly, a large house, with a sprawling yard, was offered to us by the Army. That, however, is another story.

Questions for today:

1) Can you recall your thirteenth home? Have you lived in that many places?

2) Have you ever felt homeless?

3) How long have you lived, with your family, in transition without your own home, your own address, your own neighborhood, your own telephone number, your own yard?

4) What does our text mean to you when it states "even the sparrow has found a home, and the swallow a nest for herself, where she may have her young?"

5) Do you like to move? What are your worst memories of a difficult move? How did God prove faithful to you and to your family?

Prayer: Dear Loving, Heavenly Father, Thank you for keeping us safe during a very difficult time in 1983. We struggled with our homelessness near our nation's Capitol. Be with those who are homeless today. Show to them the graciousness and kindness that you demonstrated to our family many years ago. Help all of us to remember that your care of us is much greater than that of the birds, many of which depend upon us for some of their care. Give to all of us sensitivities to those who are moving and experiencing myriad feelings of uncertainty and dread. Especially be with the many military families who must constantly make moves and adjust to new situations. Continue to build within us a trust in you so that when the hard times come; and surely they will, we will patiently wait upon you. In the loving name of Jesus, the Lord of our lives, the Creator of all who cares even for sparrows, Amen.

Day #26
"The Persistent Prodigal"
by Charles J. Carlson

—ww—

Biblical Theme: God loves us, even when we run away from him. He longs for us to come back to live in harmony with him. It is only then that we will find true peace.

Scripture for today: Read Luke 15:11-31 for the whole story.

Luke 15: 17-20,32 "When he came to his senses, he said, 'How many of my father's hired men have food to spare, and here I am starving to death! I will set out and go back to my father and say to him: Father, I have sinned against heaven and against you. I am no longer worthy to be called your son; make me like one of your hired men'. So he got up and went home to his father. But while he was still a long way off, his father saw him and was filled with compassion for him; and he ran to his son, threw his arms around him and kissed him. Then his father said, we had to celebrate and be glad, because this brother of yours was dead and is alive again; he was lost and is found."

When I was a little boy, I learned to read at a very early age. I loved any of the stories that were read to me. I was no stranger to the Golden Books series. One endearing story I remember was of a Collie dog that rescued a mother cat and her kittens after the mother cat had been struck by a car and left by the roadside for dead. Lassie placed the cat on an old coat and dragged her to the safety of the barnyard.

He then brought each of the kittens home, one by one, by the scruff of their little necks. So I always wanted to have a 'Lassie' but never did. I did however get to own 'Laddie'!

I'm a sucker for those bargain ads in the paper or those tacky 3x5 cards on the bulletin board at the grocery store. I'll stop by them nearly every time as I don't want a real bargain to pass me by. One day, when I was at our small town bank, I noticed an advertisement and picture of a beautiful Collie dog. The owners were moving out of state and they wanted their dog to live out his years on the farm. I quickly made my way back into the bank and called their number. Before the day was out, we were the proud owners of Laddie. He truly was a beautiful and well-mannered animal. I thought we hit it off perfectly. I felt that our family could meet his every need and provide for him as well as any family could. Knowing some of my history with dogs, I'm sure it would be hard to imagine that there could be any dog who wouldn't want the opportunity to live with me. We set out to prove to Laddie that he'd have a great life with us.

We kept him locked up for a few days in the barn. We spent lots of time playing with him and making sure he had all his needs met. He seemed totally comfortable with us. After several days we allowed him to graduate to his new dog house and fenced in yard. He seemed quite content with us and we had quickly fallen in love with him.

Near the end of his second week as a 'Carlson', he disappeared. His story differs some from the story of the prodigal in the Bible, for he didn't take any of our possessions with him and he didn't leave us with an inheritance to squander. Nonetheless he was gone. We looked for him for a couple of days and then put a small ad in the local newspaper. We were all quite upset and I feared the worst. I was almost certain that someone had spotted him in our yard, had noticed what a beautiful dog he was and simply stolen him. I had even heard of this happening to other people in our community.

There had been several strange disappearances of pets and some of these 'lost' dogs had ended up at the university as medical research projects. We got no response to our ad.

One of my friends suggested that we drive the twelve miles back to the farm from which Laddie had come. That seemed rather stupid to me, but since he'd said it in front of the family, I felt obligated to try. So I jumped into the pickup and made the trip. As I drove, I took the opportunity to check the fields and ditches along the way, but there was no sign of Laddie. When I pulled into the farmyard I was shocked to find Laddie patiently waiting on the back porch of his former home. He acted like he owned the place. Now really he wasn't a prodigal, he was just the opposite...he was simply going back home. He didn't realize it, but his former family had moved away. They had become prodigals and subsequently there was nothing left for him on the farm. But still he waited. I could picture him having been there for at least a couple of days now. I'm sure he had patiently sat in the driveway, waiting for cars and pickups to go by and anxiously anticipating his beloved family's return.

He looked tired and hungry. He almost seemed relieved to see me and he didn't seem to mind my putting him back into my pickup and heading home again. When we returned, I repeated the same cycle of reintroducing him to our family and once again, he handled his transition well. It wasn't long until he was free to run in the yard and enjoy farm life with few restrictions. His favorite spot to view the world was our driveway. To my surprise however, within a month, he vanished again. This time I wasn't as worried. I waited a couple of days and then repeated the trip to his former home. There he was waiting expectantly in his old driveway.

Thankfully, this time when we went back to our home, it finally became his home and he never bothered trying to leave again. He must have realized that he was loved by our family and it just wasn't going to get any better than this!

Laddie lived with us for several years until we too had to move out of state and into a city. At that point, we could have brought him along with us, but I wanted to honor his former owner's wishes for Laddie to live out his days while enjoying rural lifestyle. I was grateful that my friend, Darryl and his family decided to offer him their farm home. Everytime that I could, I'd stop in and check on him. Often I would find him lying comfortably in their driveway. I always wondered what he remembered, what he thought about and what he might have yearned for.

His patiently waiting in those driveways reminds me of the prodigal's father in the Bible story for today. He would likely go out to the end of his driveway or walkway and look all ways for as far as he could see. I'm sure he was just hoping and praying that something in his son's heart would change and that his beloved son would return to him. I'm sure that his ritual was a painful part of each and every day. It is wonderful to see his kind of faith rewarded with a happy ending.

I know what it is like to have a prodigal. I have a prodigal daughter, not a son. I don't know the answers to why she has gone away. But I too longingly yearn for her return. I wait for whatever change needs to happen in her mind and heart. I believe one day she will come back. I don't know where she is, but God does. I must simply trust Him to care for her as I no longer have that opportunity. I have to go on with my life.

I am thankful that God sees every one of us and is faithfully waiting for us to come into a right relationship with him. While He waits, He is making a wonderful place for us to live in peace and harmony with him. He desires for all of us to be with him for eternity. He wants us to enjoy everything that He has prepared. If we will but turn around and come back to him, he will gladly welcome us home. He is waiting patiently for each of us. He wants to celebrate with us that we have returned to the One who loves us like no other.

Questions for today:

1) Are you running from God or from family who loves you? What would it take in order for you to come back to God or to reunite with your family?

2) Do you think the pleasures that are offered to you in this world can provide you with lasting happiness, joy and peace? Do the people you are now with love you, just for being you, or for some other reason?

3) Is there someone in your family that is a prodigal son or daughter? Do you think of them often? Do you pray for their safety and for them to return?

4) Would you celebrate their coming back home to you or would you or others in your family simply not be able to forgive them for having been away?

Prayer: Dear Heavenly Father, I thank you and praise you that you love each of us. You want all of us to live in harmony and peace with you. Your perfect will is that we are able to live in harmony and peace with our earthly families as well. Today Lord, perhaps some of us are running from you or from the family that loves us. Heal our hearts and protect us until we can get safely back home. Lord, perhaps some of us are experiencing the unwelcome pains of having a prodigal son or daughter. Help us to continue to trust that You will care for them, even when we cannot. Lastly, Lord, some of us may already be having the opportunity or may someday get the opportunity to reintroduce our prodigal back into our family, our friends or our church family. Help us to be gracious and kind, just like you taught us to be. Help us truly to welcome them back with open arms and to celebrate with them their safe return to us. In Jesus' precious name we pray, Amen!

Day#27
"In Wrath, Remember Mercy"
by Chaplain (COL)-R Harold T. Carlson

—⟋⟍—

Biblical Theme: Just as we yearn for God's mercy to offset his righteous wrath, we fathers must show our children mercy when we are angry.

Scripture for today:
Habakkuk 3:2 "O Lord, I have heard thy speech, and was afraid: O Lord, revive thy work in the midst of the years, in the midst of the years make known; in wrath remember mercy."

I love him dearly. Just this weekend as Judy and I drove up the long driveway to our spacious farm dwelling, as it neared midnight, I saw it. There it sat near the front steps. It was the Bub's car. My heart leapt. My near clone, my second born son Nels had come home. He had only left nine days earlier to go to Midwestern Baptist Theological Seminary in Kansas City, Missouri. But, he wasn't dropping out. No...he simply had a window in time, on Super Bowl Weekend, and decided he would make the near four-hour drive and surprise us.

Have you heard that likes often clash? Nels and I don't really conflict that much but occasionally we do clash. He is a most remarkable son. He is my hunting mentor. He has abilities to rival the early Native Americans as a hunter. While he harvested five deer this year, I have struck out. In spite of that, I take some pleasure in having introduced him to the love of the outdoors. But he also has an uncanny ability to sense when the animals are out and waiting for him.

Years ago we got word from the Walter Reed Army Medical Center's Housing Office that 1726 Linden Lane was available. It was 1984. This was a remarkable, large, two-story house at the convergence of two roads. Across the street was the PX (Post Exchange) and the Commissary (Food store for the military). The location was the quaint and historic Forest Glen. This enclave boasted numerous homes with international design and flavor. At one time the property had been a casino. Later it was a girls' school. Then, the Army obtained it and made it into government quarters. Our home had, at one time, been the dwelling of the Commanding General. Right from our driveway was a long and winding, narrow road that lead to Rock Creek Parkway. This rather long trail went from north of Silver Spring, Maryland all the way to Mount Vernon, some forty miles to the south. Our little road was a tributary leading down to this pathway.

One evening the boys, Kristian, age 4 and one-half and Nels, age two were sitting with me in the enclosed porch. Here, we had our nice hide-a-bed and our television. I was enjoying time with the boys and also shining my military boots. I had my Kiwi polish out and had placed it on the back of the couch. I thought it was out of reach of little hands and I found myself watching the television show more than keeping an attentive eye on little Nels. I looked up, and to my surprise and frustration, Nels had put his little hand into the black shoe polish. I was upset. Worst of all, he had smeared some of the black stuff on the nearly new couch. I went to the kitchen and got what I needed to clean him and try to remove the polish from the couch. I made some significant progress. Then, we got back into the same routine.

Then it happened. He did it again. I was furious. I remember losing my temper and shouting at Nels. His little eyes looked so sad and I was so very mad. At the time I didn't want to think of him but only of the problem he was causing me. Still, I remember, to this day, those sad eyes and his yearning for mercy.

Fathers, do you sometimes get too angry? Do you ever treat your children with more wrath than mercy? That night I did. I still regret it. Oh, Nels recovered. But I still regret that I, a grown, strong father, would be so mad at such a little guy.

My 'Nooch Man', 'Bubba Dee', 'Nelsie Welsie Wooser', 'Noochie', is dearer to me than words can express. Just tonight we finished our twenty-ninth game of chess. We began our rivalry almost five months ago. If I can get him to play one more game before he leaves on Monday, and if I win, we will be tied. Why do I mention this? Really, I am only highlighting my love and relationship with my son. He was my answer to my wife's desire to adopt!

The night after Christmas in 1981 Nels began his life. Oh we didn't know that he would be a boy or that he would be born on September 14th, 1982 but God did. What I do know is that God wants me to remember mercy. He wants me to see a transgression, through His eyes, and never lose my temper as I did at 1726 Linden Lane, Silver Spring, Maryland in Forest Glen where we lived over twenty-three years ago.

By the way Lord, thanks for Nels' surprise visit. It is a pure delight. Is that your way of showing to Judy and to me some of your mercy as we adjust to our life here in Huggins, Missouri without this unique and dearly loved son?

Questions for today:

1) We have had fourteen houses. Have you ever had a fourteenth? Describe it.

2) Have you ever lost your temper with one of your children? What did you learn from that?

3) How has God recently shown His mercy to you? What do you think about God's wrath and mercy? How do the two intertwine and make sense together?

4) Is there some work that God wants to revive within you at this time? If so, what is it? In what area of your life do you need God's mercy most today?

Prayer: Dear Lord, Thank you for the special gift of Nels Nathanael Carlson. Be with him now as he embarks upon the challenging journey of seminary. Help him to be strong and to find the right balance of work, people and play. Thank you for the sad memory of his tender, little eyes when he got black shoe polish on our nice couch. I'm sorry I was so mad at him. Thank you for the wonderful memories that Nels has forged with me, with my wife Judy and with our family. In your kindness and mercy, bring to him the right woman for his life at just the right time. May he make You his first love. Keep him strong and prepare his heart for work as a United States Army Chaplain. In your most holy and righteous name, even the name of Jesus Christ, I pray. Amen.

Day #28
"Dare To Be Different"
by Charles J. Carlson

—ⱮⱮ—

Biblical Theme: God called many of his followers to do some seemingly crazy things. He might also call us to do things that don't always make sense to the world around us. If God calls us, the results will ultimately produce positive spiritual fruit.

Scripture for today:
Joshua 1:9 "Have I not commanded you? Be strong and courageous. Do not be terrified; do not be discouraged, for the Lord your God will be with you wherever you go."

Joshua 24:15 "But as for me and my household, we will serve the Lord."

Romans 12:2 "Do not conform any longer to the pattern of this world, but be transformed by the renewing of your mind. Then you will be able to test and approve what God's will is...his good, pleasing and perfect will."

Despite all the tragedies that we have had with our pets, it shouldn't surprise you to know that we continued to be pet lovers. There is a lesson in and of itself in that. Those we love may cause us sorrow, grief and pain...but if we believe and practice our faith, we'll continue to love... no matter what the cost. We are often challenged to behave differently from the world around us.

Our dog Pebbles was different than any other pet we'd ever owned. My first wife Mary and our daughter Kirsten probably were influenced by the movie '101 Dalmations'. Now that probably wasn't anything much different from the multitudes of other families, who at the time that movie became popular, flocked out to pet stores to buy those cute little Dalmation puppies. What was really different for us was that Pebbles would need to be almost totally a 'house dog'. She wouldn't fair very well outside in the Minnesota cold.

She would also be different in that she would influence us to do things for her that we'd never done for any other pet we'd had. You see, she was the most adorable puppy. She immediately won us over with her charm and beauty. I still have pictures of her that make me laugh. I also have a 5x7 postcard that really sums up her life with us and that card is the impetus for the title of this devotional. On the postcard, a group of Dalmations is gathered for a 'family photo'. One of the pups shows up for the photo wearing some multi-colored eyeglass wear and has dyed its spots different colors. The slogan at the top of the card reads… "Dare to be Different". Honestly, it seemed to be Pebbles' life goal.

Pebbles really belonged to Kirsten and Mary. She seemed to understand that from the start. She enjoyed being with them more much than with me or our son. This in itself was different. Our family pets in the past had always seemed to take to us all equally. She seemed to know that she was serving a multipurpose in our household and that her main mission was to make them happy. Her presence was a cure-all for those days of depression and a welcome substitute for the pet we had all had to leave behind when we moved from South Dakota to Minnesota. Yet she was different from any other pet we'd had, in that she was a very hard dog to house train. We nearly gave up on her, but she finally got it. In every other way, she carried herself with such elegance and grace, but she was very stubborn and independent. I can still remember her riding in the car so proudly with us or seeing her play on the trampoline with Kirsten, Chad and their friends. She loved to bounce with them. That too was a bit different!

She could be the sweetest dog with our family or with the neighbor kids, but then sometimes she'd let a side of her personality show through that was frightening. She would become possessive of her space or more accurately 'our space'. She wouldn't be content to stay in the kennel or the garage when we needed her to stay there. She'd bark and claw and scratch until we'd give in. That was different for us too as normally we were in control of our pets, not the other way around.

On Sunday evenings, we hosted one of several small Bible study groups in our home. Pebbles had to be around or she'd make so much noise that we couldn't think or converse. The only thing that calmed her was to let her be in the kitchen while we talked, studied and prayed in the living room. This arrangement was different because in order to make that happen, we had to close two rather large openings between the living room and the kitchen/dining room. So we'd move our couch in front of the largest one and then put up a child-proof gate in the other doorway. We thought we had the problem solved.

Pebbles had some endearing ways but her attitude and personality caused her to do something that became her eventual demise with our family. One Sunday night, she decided that lying contently on the kitchen floor wasn't enough. So without any warning, she jumped up on the back of the couch and bit one of the ladies in our Bible study. It wasn't a severe bite but it was significant enough to leave a mark and create quite a situation. Pebbles' behavior was different, but not in a good way. It certainly wasn't a 'God ordained' moment.

In the days ahead, she became increasingly moody and started 'nipping' at others inside and outside the family. We then heard from her birth owners that they had had a similar problem with another one of their pups from a previous litter. The recommendation was that Pebbles needed more space, more freedom and fewer people coming in/out of her life. With great regret, our daringly different Dalmation was sent to a new home.

As I stated in the beginning of this devotional, God sometimes calls us to 'be different'. When it is God that is doing the calling, it is a remarkable thing and we'll likely see positive fruit from our efforts. We might also have some opposition to what we are doing or to the message we are attempting to share with others. But when we launch out on our own to be different (like Pebbles did), we can cause ourselves and others real harm. If God isn't calling us, then we'll likely be just weird or disturbing to those around us. Our behaviors will produce little positive fruit and perhaps do more harm than good. It is very important for us to know and understand what the good, perfect and acceptable will of God in every situation really is. If we jump out to be 'different', just for the sake of being different, we will be ineffective or much worse. When Pebbles followed her own sinful ways, she quickly became a detriment instead of a blessing.

Pebbles intrigue with our family was that she was such a different pet than what we'd ever had. It was like God had called her to our family for a special time with a special purpose. But Pebbles' strong will and subsequent obnoxious personality traits served no redeeming purpose.

God wants us to act differently than the world around us acts and reacts to this life and to the life to come. But he never calls us to be 'weird, obnoxious or biting' in our words or in our conduct with others. He wants us to be conformed to His ways and then He wants us to be transformed into His likeness so that we can be effective in our relationships to those both inside and outside of His kingdom. May we be able to say that with God's help, we and our entire household will serve the Lord. May we be 'different' from the world but in a positive, life-giving way. Come on, I dare you!!

Questions for today:

1) Have you ever had a pet that was strong-willed? How about a child?

2) What was the strangest behavior you have ever observed another person exhibit? Do you think they were obeying God, themselves or something/someone else?

3) Has God ever asked you to do something the world would consider different? What was it? Have you seen any positive fruit from it?

4) Why is it so hard to be 'different'? What does it mean to you and your family to 'not be conformed to this world but to be transformed'?

Prayer: Dear Heavenly Father, help us to understand what your good, acceptable and perfect will is for our lives. Help us to know the difference between the voices that pull at our heart, mind and spirit. Help us only to listen to your voice as we want to be 'different' in a positive way from the world, but we don't want to be strange or deceived. Help us to have the courage we need in our lives to do positive things for you, our great and loving God. In Jesus' precious name we pray, Amen.

Day #29
"The Life of a Stranger"
by Chaplain (COL)-R Harold T. Carlson

—ʍ—

Biblical Theme: There are times when we, God's children, feel like strangers. We must remember that to God, we are always known. We must also understand that for sojourners, there will be times when we are seen as strangers on earth.

Scripture for today:
Exodus 2: 16-22 "Now the priest of Midian had seven daughters: and they came and drew water, and filled the troughs to water their father's flock. And when they came to Reuel their father, he said, How is it that ye are come so soon today? And they said, 'An Egyptian delivered us out of the hand of the shepherds, and also drew water enough for us, and watered the flock'. And he said unto his daughters, 'And where is he?' Why is it that ye have left the man? Call him, that he may eat bread.' And Moses was content to dwell with the man: and he gave Moses Zipporah his daughter as his wife. And she bare him a son, and he called his name Gershom: for he said, 'I have been a stranger in a strange land.'

I was a stranger in a strange land too. How odd that my little Annalisa saw me as just such a person? For nearly ten years Judy and I had noticed this farm place. It was seven miles north of Beresford, South Dakota on Old Highway 77. It had such beautiful Scotch Pine trees. It had a wind shelter belt and it boasted nice outbuildings too. The two-story, large white house had an open, front porch, and an upstairs as well as a spacious, unfinished basement. Why could we ever have this place and how would we ever occupy it since God had called us into the military? In spite of these circumstances, Tillman and his wife retired from their farm. They sold most of the quarter section of land. But, the six plus acres and the farm home and buildings were available. This was in the early spring of 1986. I had been selected by the Army to attend the Chaplains' Advanced Course in Fort Monmouth, New Jersey. The quarters were small and we were a family of eight. We did an unusual thing. We made an offer of $42,000 for the property. What was more remarkable is that the Nelsons took it. Somehow, we felt we belonged there. Judy's maiden name was Nelson. Why shouldn't the property go to a person who was at least 'half-Nelson'?

With my PCS leave and travel time, coupled with time for going to a denominational conference in Boulder, Colorado, I had nearly six weeks to pretend that I was a civilian. We returned from the church event and quickly got settled into our new 'farm' life. We all loved it. But then, it happened. The day came when I had to go and leave the family for over six months. It was a most challenging time.

I can still hardly believe it. During those months of life apart, I got special air fares and used much ingenuity. I would buy a ticket for a Saturday flight. I would then go to Newark, New Jersey and find a flight to Minneapolis and then on to Sioux Falls. I often got a round trip ticket for $69.00. That got me to the Twin Cities. I still had two hundred and seventy miles to go. This second leg often cost more than the long one to the east coast. I always, with much suspense, used my ticket to go 'Standby' the evening before I had a legitimate claim to a seat and a ride to Minneapolis.

What I didn't factor into these delightful escapades to home was that my little daughter, Annalisa, only fifteen to eighteen months old, did not remember me. My visits were about a month apart. Each time I came home she was hesitant to come to me. Who was I? I felt like a stranger in a strange land with her. Oh, the other family members made me feel right at home and I was. But Anna, she did not get it. Who was this guy who came for two nights, tried to live a month within those days and then left? To her, I remained a stranger.

I wonder what it must have been like for Moses. He left everything familiar and went to live in another culture on the back side of the desert. What sustained him? How did he make sense of such a pilgrim experience? I think that the same God who sustained me and comforted my mind and heart was the same God who provided for him, gave him a home and even a wife and children.

I think of Jesus' powerful words, "A stranger and you took me in." A stranger...Life as a military officer can be most challenging. It is not easy to leave a wife whom we love, children who need a father, and toddlers who often forget that we are even related. Serving God and Country comes with a high price tag at times.

Our sojourn in South Dakota was a precious wrinkle in time. In reality, although we owned the property for ten years, those seven months were the only ones in which we occupied our home and lived in that locale. Many memories, such as living only one quarter of a mile from my brother and his family, living only seven miles from my mom and step-father, only nine miles from my older sister, her husband Paul and my niece, and finally only thirty-eight miles from another brother and his family, all made this time different than all other times of our military career. But, I will never forget the sad ache that I felt when little Anna did not recognize me as her father.

This now grown daughter begins her Student Teaching next week at Barclay College, in Haviland, Kansas. She is a soul-mate with me. As she grew, she was the one who would see me working in the hot sun and, unprompted, come with a glass of water and a towel for my brow. There is no problem in our knowing our relationship now. Thank God that my time as a stranger in a strange land was short.

Questions for today:

1) Have you ever lived in fifteen places? That is a lot of moves! Was it hard to leave that place?

2) Do you remember a time when your children did not recognize you? How did you handle this? How did you feel?

3) Do you ever think about our life as Christians? In particular, the writer of Hebrews call us pilgrims, strangers, travelers on earth with no permanent dwelling. What do you think about that?

4) Do you ever pray for military families who move so often? Would you do that now?

Prayer: Dear Lord, Thank you that we are never strangers to You if we have Jesus as the Savior of our lives. Help us to be sensitive and caring to people who are new to our community. Especially be with military families and with children of officers and enlisted men and women. Help them to take Your hand, hold tightly to your grip and never let go. Bring to them loving and caring people who will take them in and make them feel that they belong. Thank you for my Annalisa. I love her so. Help her as she does her Student Teaching and lead her to the Godly man who will find the treasure, like no other, that she represents. These things I pray in your Holy and Righteous Name, You, the Wonderful Counselor, Amen.

Day#30
"Colonel Bradley, the Faithful Dog that We Divorced"

by Charles J. Carlson

—ɷ—

Biblical Theme: We need to honor our relationships with our pets, but more importantly our relationships with our families.

Scripture for today: Ps. 68:6 "God sets the lonely in families."

Pr. 12:10 "A righteous man cares for the needs of his animal".

Mal. 2:16 "I hate divorce, says the Lord God of Israel."

Matt. 19:6 "Therefore, what God has joined together, let man not separate."

Early December of 2000 ushered in another cold and blustery winter night in rural Minnesota. As I traveled back from Willmar to Hutchinson, there were times I could barely see the road. I had been on another 'car repairing' mission for my daughter, Kirsten. This time it was the starter. It seemed that the car that had served her so well since she was 16, was now falling apart at the seams in her first year of cosmetology school at Willmar Technical College.

I sure wasn't looking for him but I'd swear to this day that it really was Bradley. Bradley was one of the coolest

187

pets ever and the last dog that I've owned. There he was, wondering along that drift laden highway, looking none too pleased with life. I quickly pulled the car over and stepped out into the frigid cold. As soon as I had opened my door, he took off down the ditch and darted out into the open field. I could barely see him sitting out there in the moonlight with the snow blowing all around him. I began calling for him. I tried everything I could but the dog didn't respond. He just sat there on the frozen ground and studied me like he was trying to remember if I was familiar or not. Unfortunately, we weren't family anymore. Just three months before, we had 'divorced' Bradley and sent him away to live with a farm family that promised to give him freedom and a great life. After I finally accepted that this dog (whether he really was Bradley or not) wasn't going to respond to me, I got back in my warm car and sped off again. I cried most of the way back to town as I questioned my earlier decision to part with my dog. I also thought about the countless number of other pets that people abandon everyday. These poor creatures are left to fend for themselves. Most of them end up along the roadside in pieces. Anyone who rids themselves of their responsibility to their pet in that way should be ashamed of themselves. It's heartless, not kind and just not right!

As you may have noticed from some of the other stories I've shared, we have had a special place in our hearts for Golden Retrievers; especially ones that are related to the dogs that other family members had. We were fortunate enough to get Bradley from my brother Tim and his family down in Missouri. Bradley had already been given his name by my nephews by the time we picked him up. I added the 'Colonel' to his name, in honor of my brother's quest to be Colonel in the United States Army. I figured that this dog would be with me through its old age. I wanted his later years to be marked by a name of special distinction. Tim became Colonel. I still wish I knew what became of Bradley.

Little Bradley was such a loving, caring pup. He traveled all the way from Missouri to Minnesota without one mess. From the first day, till the day I divorced him from our family, I never once regretted our times together. As you may have guessed, we lived in town. It isn't always the easiest thing to have a large pet indoors and although we house-trained him and let him have the run of our home, he really enjoyed the outdoors. It was after his first winter with us that we made a decision that Bradley was going to be an outdoor dog.

We still had a large doghouse that I moved with us from the farm in South Dakota years before. I made a large dog run for Bradley, just off of our deck. He seemed very pleased with life there. I even painted his name on the doghouse so he'd feel right at home. I know that others in the family and the neighborhood children loved playing with him. He liked jumping with them on the trampoline. I loved throwing him a tennis ball or a Frisbee; we could entertain each other for hours. On rare occasions, I'd take him in the van to the lake or river; he was a great swimmer. My favorite times with him were late at night, when most of the town was quiet. Either I or my wife and I together would take him about four blocks away to the walking path that went all around the school grounds. It was there that Bradley was the most 'free'. I would take him off his leash and let him run around on the practice football fields. He could fly like the wind and he didn't seem to tire. Sometimes I would spend more time out there than others, but each time, when I called, he'd come bounding back to me seemingly just grateful for having had the opportunity to be out of his cage. I was amazed at how obedient he was. Most of his days were spent just waiting out in his cage...waiting to eat...waiting for someone to play with...just waiting for some special attention. He was always faithful, even when we weren't. In truth, I'm sure Bradley was lonely.

It was a couple years later after the traumatic loss of my pastoral employment that I noticed that I spent less and less time with Bradley. I was forced into a seventy mile commute (each way) to attempt to provide for my family. It wasn't a pleasant experience and often when I got home late in the evening, I didn't feel like I had the energy to go on our daily walks. My weekends were taken up with trying to reconnect with family, being a help around the house and needing to take care of our lawn. As I look back, it was a poor decision to give up on those special times with our dog. Eventually, I began to see my time with Bradley as much more of a chore instead of a joy. Something had to give.

It took only one ad in the newspaper and interviewing two interested families for us to find Bradley another home. I chose the 'farm family' because I had great memories of my life on the farm and I wanted Bradley running free. Our 'doggie divorce' was quickly arranged as I gave the new owner the dog run, the dog house, the dog dishes, the leashes and the walking chain. Within a week, I had repaired the yard where the kennel sat and laid down new sod. Although I visibly removed any sign of Bradley from my sight, I've never removed him from my memory. I'm sure he didn't understand what happened. I'm sure he missed me as much as I missed him. I'm sure that he hated his 'divorce' from us. I made no plans to go to visit him; I figured it would just be too painful. I take some comfort in thinking that maybe God, who cares about how we care for our animals, cared enough about Bradley to set him into a new, more faithful family.

'Divorcing' a pet is one thing. But divorce for humans is much more traumatic. I know we've all heard horror stories about divorce. It's no wonder that God doesn't like it. If divorcing Bradley felt this bad, I didn't want to know what real divorce feels like. But I do, for it happens far too often and far too easily, with shock waves that reverberate through families, friends, churches and communities. In fact, I know of a man who went to work one morning and when he got home in the late evening, all his personal possessions had been moved from their bedroom to the basement and his wife declared that they were now separated! Because that man couldn't accept this living arrangement, he moved out and ever so quickly, a painful stress-filled divorce followed. He never had another meaningful conversation with either his wife or his daughter. Without a hint of regret, his daughter separated him from herself and his two grandchildren. It was amazing that in this horrific story, even his former in-laws didn't care enough to reach out to help them. His is the most troubling story of divorce I've ever known. He had done nothing to deserve such treatment. He had been faithful to his wife and his family in every way. He must have felt as hurt and confused as my dear dog Bradley did. Neither one of them knew what hit them! I pray for that man that God will restore him, heal his heart and fulfill his promises to him, like the one that says 'God sets the lonely in families'. May this truth be so real for him and for each one of you who needs to recover from the trauma of divorce, death, grief and loss. God can make a way, where there seems to be no way!

Questions for today:

1) Have you ever had to separate yourself from your pet? Is there anything about that experience that you would do differently? Do you recognize that some pets are just better off with new families?

2) Are you lonely? Have you prayed that God would 'set' you in a family or grouping of people who love and care for you?

3) Are you divorced or do you know someone who is? If so, would you pray for them and reach out to them? They need comfort, acceptance and to be reassured that although God doesn't like divorce...He still loves them!

4) If you are divorced, what miracle would it take for you to get back together? Is that anything you'd even consider or have you moved on and rebuilt your life? Do you ever think of them? Can you ask God to bless and forgive them? Will you give your bitterness and disappointment to God and let Him heal your heart and mind?

Prayer: Dear Heavenly Father, thank you for loving us and forgiving us, no matter what. Thank you for the happy memories of our pets. They have meant so much to us in our lives. Forgive us if we've ever abandoned our pet along the side of a road. We knew better but we did it anyway. Lord, help us never to love our pets so much more than we do people. Help us not to become so involved in caring for our pets that we miss caring for our families or miss seeing the needs of people around us. More importantly, help us to reach out to those people who seem to be lonely and in need of friendship. Help us not to be judgmental towards those who have had to endure the pain of divorce. Help us to be willing to give you all our past and in doing so, trust you for a bright future as members of the family of God. Amen!

Day #31
"I Was Sick and You Visited Me"
by Chaplain (COL)-R Harold T. Carlson

—m—

Bibical Theme: God is pleased when we care for the sick.

Scriptures for today: Matthew 25:35-36 "For I was hungry, and you gave me meat; I was thirsty and you gave me drink. I was a stranger, and you took me in. Naked, and you clothed me; I was sick, and you visited me. I was in prison, and you came unto me."

Job 1:21 "Naked came I out of my mother's womb, and naked shall I return thither: the Lord gave, and the Lord hath taken away; blessed be the name of the Lord."

She really wanted to live. Judy and I bought 'Heidi', a sort of 'hammerhead looking' Charolais heifer about five months ago. She was a 'bargain'. Truthfully, I thought we had made a good investment. With the forty-four dollars for recent medicine, and the free vet care that I gave to her for twelve days; we each had about seventy-five dollars in our investment. I had never given such care to any animal. She seemed alert, she ate and drank; she held up her head and ears but…with the cold, and the extended time on the ground, she simply could not walk. Yesterday, my son Kristian and I made a sling for her. We suspended her, put a platform under her and allowed her to move her legs without the strain of trying to stand. That apparatus might

195

have helped initially. In the end, which Judy and I observed this morning when we went to feed the horses and cattle, she had moved slightly forward, shifted in the sling and wedged her head against the building.

Did all this happen at our sixteenth home? No. I simply had to fast forward across the years and many of our homes to our present dwelling. The next one in chronological order, 425 Glacier in Fairbanks, Alaska where we spent five and one-half years, has enough memories for an entire devotional book. That home, and many since, will have to await a later disclosure. Here, at 9619 Highway AH, Huggins, Missouri is the site of this writing where I am reminding myself and my readers of Jesus' words, "I was sick and you visited me".

Last week I called a retired chaplain friend. He is awaiting another kidney. As his current 'new' kidney is failing, he goes thirty-five miles three times each week to Lebanon, Missouri. There, for four hours, he undergoes dialysis. For a time he tried to visit with others or read. Now, he goes, gets hooked up, pulls a cover over his head and goes to sleep. He looks ashen gray. We were going to lunch. He would be my guest. We talked of many things: his son Justin, now an Enlisted Military Police Soldier, his wife Pam and her desire to take a leave of absence to spend more time with him, his two grandchildren, his desire to visit his aging father and relatives in Florida and his time as a chaplain and earlier, as a Corpsman, in Viet Nam. Recently he had been dreaming about his life as a Corpsman.

I attempted to appear unaffected, in a negative way, by his frailty and loss of appetite. I tried to reassure and to encourage him. As I dropped him off at Pick Elementary School, at Fort Leonard Wood, Missouri where Pam teaches, Russ said, "Thanks for coming all this way to take me to lunch". I had driven about forty-five miles to be with him. I replied, "Russ, you are my friend. I value you. Coming this far is nothing compared to your worth and my desire to spend some time with you. I'm just sorry that I have waited so long". I am reminded of Jesus' words, "I was sick and you visited me."

I certainly visited our sick calf Heidi. I injected her with Vitamin B. I used a whole bottle. I nearly emptied a costly bottle of Banamine and another 'mycine' drug too. I fed and watered her. Both Judy and I often checked on her and prayed for her. I thought she might live. Why? Really, I linked her hopes to Judy's prayers and her part of the investment. This was her only calf on the place.

Our life here at our farm home is filled with activities. Recently, we have worked diligently to recover from the memorable and historic ice storm of 2007. We have taken numerous trips around the property on our four-wheelers and checked on the livestock daily. We have hosted guests, including a weekly Bible study and numerous events for Judy's lady friends. But, for me, the event that has caused me the greatest pause has been this death of Heidi. Indeed, her strange life and death are still causing me to ponder. It is rare for a sick animal to live for twelve days without being able to stand and move about. I have mused as to the reason why she lived so long. For me, the only real answer comes from our second scripture reading for today.

Two days ago 'Jenks' was born. Another bargain, an old black white face cow gave birth to this bull calf. He is a 'cutie' indeed. When Judy and I attended Trinity College in Deerfield, Illinois in the mid-sixties, the Chicago Cubs had a very talented pitcher named Ferguson Jenkins. As this is Black History Month, and he was Black, we decided to name our calf after him. We just shortened the name to Jenks. In God's Providence this little creature came two days before our enfeebled heifer died. So, today, with Job, we can say, "The Lord giveth and the Lord taketh away, blessed be the Name of the Lord."

I have no malice, no ill will and no anger towards God for Heidi's death. I do wonder why she lived so long considering her symptoms and weakened state. But, I also think of our human journey. In truth, only our relationships with people can yield results that give ultimate pleasure to God. While I spent hours with our sick animal, I spent only a couple of hours with my friend Russ. I think there is a spiritual lesson in that for me. I believe that times for pause and for pondering are gifts from our Creator. My desire is to refine my current priorities. I need to allow God to move me to spend time on those things and persons that matter the most to Him. I'm sorry that Heidi died. But, for me, she did not die in vain.

Questions for today:

1) Have you ever had a sick animal? Did it recover from its illness? Did it die?

2) Do you have any persons somewhat near to you that are currently sick? Have you visited them? Do you recall what the people whom Jesus addressed answered when he said to them, "I was sick and you visited me"?

3) What event in your life has recently caused you to pause and to ponder?

4) To what can you and your family say, "The Lord giveth and the Lord taketh away, blessed be the Name of the Lord"?

Prayer: Dear Lord, I confess to some sadness today. Heidi died. She seemed so trusting and perseverant. I did all that I could do for her and yet; she is gone! Thanks for the memory of her strange life. She was sort of 'half of a calf' all of her life. I think of my friend Russ today. He needs a new kidney. His system also needs to accept it. He needs new strength and new hope. I pray that you will touch him and be with him today as he goes again to dialysis. Help me to remember the sick and to visit them. Thank you for health. It is such a great gift. Thank you for our farm place, our retirement home. We like it a lot but we like and love you more. If you want this to be our place to live now, we rejoice. If not, we give it today and everyday back to You and await new marching orders. Help us to join Job in an attitude that blesses you in loss or gain. In the Holy Name of Jesus Christ our Lord, we pray, Amen.

Conclusion

—ɷ—

Is it really over? Over two years ago Chuck and I agreed that we would write a devotional book together. He has had over thirty dogs and our family has lived in nearly thirty places! Well, we've done it. My sixteen are complete and nearly two months ago he finished his last one. I have enjoyed the challenge and the walk down memory lane.

I want to address that walk for a few moments. Each of us is forging a history. When I spoke with my son Nels the other day he said, "Dad, whether this thing sells or not, I'm excited. You are leaving our family a legacy. You are telling our story." I accept that but I think it is only half of what I want to convey. Maybe, it is only a third. The second third is this: "God is the main actor in each of our families' lives". Are we in tune with that? Are we taking time to remind ourselves of His activity and love towards us? The last third is this, "You too have a story to tell"!

As I have paused to recall our journey, I invite you, after you have read our devotionals, pondered the questions and prayed, to consider doing something very exciting. Sit down at your desk, your computer, your work station and begin. At least do one devotional. You may be a family that has only moved once or maybe never. You may be a family that has moved fifty times. Whatever, would you take time to recount one of those homes, one of those stories and leave your own legacy?

Finally, I am a Soldier. I am an Army Officer. I am a United States Army Military Chaplain. Would you pray for our military? We are in war today. The stakes for freedom are high. We can't bring ultimate freedom. Only Jesus can do that. But, we in our nation's freedom fight, need Jesus. Our families need Jesus. We need your prayers and we need God's mercy.

May God bless you and your family today. Happy reading! Happy pondering! 'Til we meet at Jesus' feet, God be with you and with us.

Sincerely,
Chaplain (COL)-R Harold (Tim) T. Carlson
United States Army Chaplain, Retired

It wasn't a race but I finished writing my portion of the devotionals first. Brother Tim however, completed his conclusion before me so his conclusion got to go first...he's always doing things first!

I hope that you have enjoyed our devotionals as much as we have enjoyed the process of birthing them. I just got off the phone with Tim and we were reminiscing about our work, start to finish. When we started this, we knew our devotional topics would be about 'dogs and houses' but we never made an exact plan of what we wanted to say or how we wanted to say it. We believed in God's help and respected each other's commitment to the task. If our book is only a means of sharing our story with our family, that's enough for us as it has been a wonderful way to tell some of our separate, but intertwining journeys.

Each of us has experienced loss in this life. God has sustained us both throughout. He deserves all glory and praise. As brother Tim's last devotional so aptly illustrated, 'the Lord gives and the Lord takes away, blessed be the name of the Lord.'

Our God is truly a God of hope, restoration and healing. As you have no doubt learned, not only from our musings about our homes and our pets, but also from your own experiences, homes and pets can influence us greatly. However, the unwanted or unexpected loss of our pets or our homes will leave impressions either positive or negative which will likely cause us to become 'bitter or better'. We thank God that in His mercy, He has helped us to see our losses and grief in light of eternity which helps us not to become bitter. He has been faithful to do for us exactly what Romans 8:28, 37-39 says which is "And we know that in all things God works for the good of those who love him, who have been called according to his purpose. In all these things we are more than conquerors through him who loved us. For I am convinced that neither death nor life, neither angels nor demons, neither the present nor the future, nor any powers, neither height nor depth, nor anything else in all creation, will be able to separate us from the love of God that is in Christ Jesus our Lord."

We wanted to encourage you with examples of God's helping us to find 'good' in some of the negative aspects of our life's journey. In doing so, our hope is that you too will find the hope, restoration and healing that you and your family needs as you give over everything to God. I couldn't have possibly imagined all the 'different hats' I'd wear in my life. You might feel the same way. Rest assured that God sees, understands and can bring good from every situation.

Although I'm not currently a pastor of a church but rather working as a mortgage loan officer, my heart is still in ministry. Where is your heart? What is the guiding force that drives you? Do you realize that God considers all of his followers to be 'ministers' in one way or another? I challenge you to find ways to let your life speak to others. God wants to use us if we are willing and open to his leading and direction.

We may be separated from those we love. We may lose our pets, our homes, our jobs, our health or a myriad of other things. However, if we love God and if we have a personal relationship with Jesus Christ, the Lord and Savior, we will never lose out on the love God has for us. That is the most important story of all.

If you've never taken the bold step of asking Jesus Christ to be the Lord and Savior of your life, why not do so today? It doesn't mean that your life will be easy and trouble free. It doesn't mean that you won't experience loss or tragedy. But it certainly means you'll be better equipped to deal with them.

The words or prayer you say will be the easiest part. Living out your new found commitment will be the challenge. Why not pray with me now and be assured that you'll have the love of God for all eternity?

Dear Heavenly Father, I need you for I am a sinner. I believe that you came into this world to save people just like me. Please forgive me for my sins that have separated me from you. I ask you Jesus to come into my heart and to be the Lord of my life. I welcome the presence and power of your Holy Spirit right now. Help me to live my life for you. I trust you not only for my salvation but I believe that you will bring other people into my life that can demonstrate Your love to me and help me to grow in my new life with You. Help me to be secure in knowing that no amount of hardship or tragedy can separate me from Your love for me, either now or forever. In Jesus' precious name, I pray, Amen.

If one person is encouraged by our devotional or one person prays a prayer of faith to receive Jesus into his or her heart, then Tim and I have achieved our goal. If you are one of those people, why not drop us an email to let us know. We'd love to hear from you.

Sincerely,
Rev. Charles J. Carlson
Blaine, MN 55449
cjcbigbaby@yahoo.com

or

Chaplain (COL)-R Harold T. Carlson
Huggins, MO 65484
norskshus@aol.com

Biography of Chaplain (COL)-R Harold Timothy Carlson

—ɯ—

Chaplain (COL)-R Harold Timothy Carlson was reared in southeastern Kentucky and graduated from Clinton High School in Iowa. He graduated from Trinity International University in 1969 and was drafted into the United States Army in 1971. He entered Sioux Falls Seminary in 1976 and graduated 'cum laude' in 1979 with a Masters of Divinity Degree. He was a National Honor Society Member in high school and selected to 'Who's Who in Colleges and Universities' in 1969 and 1979.

He entered the Army as a chaplain in 1980. His tours include Special Projects Officer for Mentoring at the Chief of Chaplain's Office in Washington, D.C., Installation Chaplain at Fort Rucker, Alabama and at Fort Leonard Wood, Missouri. His awards include the Legion of Merit, the Meritorious Service Medal with six Oak Leaf Clusters and the De Fleury Ribbon (Bronze) from the Corps of Engineers. He was the first chaplain for the Corps and wrote their Official Prayer in 1999. He was honored for his writing by the Corps with the Quill Award and by the Army receiving the Keith L. Ware Award.

He is married to the former Judy Raye Nelson. They have six children and ten grandchildren. He is a member of the Evangelical Free Church of America. Besides writing,

Tim enjoys cattle raising, four-wheeling, golf, tennis, traveling, verbal sparring and the great game of Rook.

Biography of Charles J. Carlson

—ɷ—

Reverend Charles J. Carlson spent his formative years in Kentucky, Iowa and South Dakota where he graduated from Beresford High School in 1974. He attended South Dakota State University before entering into a farming career. Some years later he followed the call of God for ministry and graduated from Sioux Falls Seminary in 1992 with Masters of Divinity and Masters of Arts Degrees. He faithfully served in pastoral ministry for eleven years. Through unexpected life circumstances he left full-time ministry and became a mortgage loan officer. Chuck enjoys many of the same sports and hobbies as his older brother Tim. In his spare time he has become a published author and a poet. He dedicates his work to God; the One who completely knows his heart.

Charles has discovered that life doesn't always turn out like he would have planned it. No matter what your life experience has been, connecting spiritually with God will bring you certain peace and a secure future. Charles is happily married to his best friend, Nicole Dawn Carlson. Charles has two incredibly gifted and much loved children, Chad and Kirsten, from his first marriage. He is also the proud grandparent of Freedom Song and Journey Spirit.

Rev. Charles J. Carlson
(Chuck)

Chaplain(COL)-R
Harold T. Carlson
(Tim)

Printed in the United States
202624BV00001B/265-315/A